DIALOGUES ON CONSTITUTIONAL ORIGINS,
STRUCTURE, AND CHANGE IN FEDERAL COUNTRIES

T0158439

A Global Dialogue on Federalism
Booklet Series
Volume I

DIALOGUES ON CONSTITUTIONAL ORIGINS, STRUCTURE, AND CHANGE IN FEDERAL COUNTRIES

EDITED BY RAOUL BLINDENBACHER
AND ABIGAIL OSTIEN

Published for

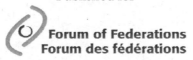

Forum of Federations
Forum des fédérations

and

iacfs
INTERNATIONAL ASSOCIATION OF
CENTERS FOR FEDERAL STUDIES

by

McGill-Queen's University Press
Montreal & Kingston · London · Ithaca

© McGill-Queen's University Press 2005
ISBN 978-0-7735-2939-7

Legal deposit first quarter 2005
Bibliothèque nationale du Québec
Reprinted 2010

Printed in Canada on acid-free paper that is 100% ancient forest free
(100% post-consumer recycled), processed chlorine free.

McGill-Queen's University Press acknowledges the support of the Canada
Council for the Arts for our publishing program. We also acknowledge
the financial support of the Government of Canada through the Book
Publishing Industry Development Program (BPIDP) for our publishing
activities.

Library and Archives Canada Cataloguing in Publication

Dialogues on constitutional origins, structure, and change in federal
    countries/edited by Raoul Blindenbacher and Abigail Ostien.

(A global dialogue on federalism booklet series; v. 1)
ISBN 978-0-7735-2939-7

    1. Constitutional law. 2. Federal government. I. Blindenbacher, Raoul
II. Ostien, Abigail J., 1971– III. Forum of Federations IV. International
Association of Centers for Federal Studies V. Series: Global dialogue on
federalism booklet series; v. 1.

JC355.D523 2005   342′.042   C2004-907327-3

This book was typeset by Interscript Inc. in 10/12 Baskerville.

Contents

Preface

This booklet explores the origins, structure, and change of federal constitutions and reflects a series of lively dialogues that occurred in Australia, Belgium, Brazil, Canada, Germany, India, Mexico, Nigeria, Russia, South Africa, Switzerland, and the United States. Those who participated in the dialogue events – both practitioners and academics – are constitutional experts in their respective countries, all presenting a diversity of viewpoints.

The content of these short articles provides the reader with a brief synopsis of each featured country's constitutional history and current challenges. The authors' words are a reflection of their own understanding of the issue and of the insights gained during the dialogue events. Among the questions explored in the articles are: what is the constitution's overall level of success, including its capacity to adapt to changing circumstances? Was the constitution created through a popular or elite process? Was it the product of vision or a series of compromises? How did the homogeneity or heterogeneity of the population affect the constitution-making process? What were the primary aims of the constitution at the time of its creation? A range of current issues are presented in the articles including: rights and republicanism, regional and social inequality, electoral, parliamentary, and senate reform, and accommodating diversities of language, culture, religion, and values. Each of the featured countries' constitutions is confronting challenges, both common and unique.

This booklet, the first in a series, is a product of a program of the Forum of Federations and the International Association of Centers for Federal Studies (IACFS) called *A Global Dialogue on Federalism*. The Global Dialogue program produces a series of booklets and corresponding books, each set featuring a different theme on federal governance.

The booklet begins with a chapter briefly explaining the Global Dialogue program structure before proceeding to the country articles, entitled "Dialogue Insights." It concludes with a chapter summarizing commonalities and differences in the featured countries. The style in which it is written, its brevity, and extra features, such as a glossary and timeline, all contribute to a publication that promotes accessibility, providing an entry point to the corresponding theme book. It is our intention that the articles presented here will serve to 'whet your appetite' for Volume I of the book, *Constitutional Origins, Structure, and Change in Federal Countries,* wherein the same authors are able to explore the topic in much greater detail.

The Global Dialogue on Federalism Series continues a tradition of Forum of Federations' publications either independently, or in partnership with other organizations. The Forum has produced a variety of books and multimedia material. Refer to the Forum's website at www.forumfed.org for more information on the Forum's publications and activities. The website also contains links to other organizations and an online library.

We would like to express our appreciation to the authors of the first theme booklet for their contributions to this volume. Special thanks are due to G. Alan Tarr for writing the final chapter, "Comparative Reflections." We wish to acknowledge the participants who took part in the twelve country events for providing a diversity of perspectives that helped to shape the articles themselves. Their names are listed at the end of the booklet. John Kincaid, Cheryl Saunders, Ronald L. Watts, and the rest of the Global Dialogue Editorial Board have offered their invaluable advice and expertise. We would also like to mention Alan Fenna and Thomas Hueglin for creating the glossary and Lise Rivet for her assistance with the timeline. We would like to acknowledge the support offered by several staff members at the Forum of Federations. They include: Rebeca Batres-Doré, Barbara Brook, Maxime Cappeliez, Rhonda Dumas, Karl Nerenberg, and Carl Stieren. Finally, we thank the staff at McGill-Queen's University Press for all of their assistance throughout the publication process.

Whether you are working in the field of federalism, a student or teacher of federalism, or simply interested in the topic, this booklet should prove to be an insightful, brief look at the origins and current status of each of the featured countries' constitutions.

Raoul Blindenbacher and Abigail Ostien, editors

DIALOGUES ON CONSTITUTIONAL ORIGINS,
STRUCTURE, AND CHANGE IN FEDERAL COUNTRIES

A Global Dialogue on Federalism

RAOUL BLINDENBACHER
AND BARBARA BROOK

This booklet is the outcome of roundtable events held in a dozen federal countries, as well as at an international comparative roundtable, all exploring the theme of "Constitutional Origins, Structure, and Change in Federal Countries," as part of the program, *A Global Dialogue on Federalism.* The Forum of Federations and the International Association of Centers for Federal Studies (IACFS) are collaborating on this program to engage participants in comparative dialogues about core themes on federalism, with the aims of learning from each other's knowledge and experience and building an international network. This article provides a brief description of the Global Dialogue program and the method that the program partners have developed in order to achieve our aims. To read more about the Global Dialogue's rationale, refer to the chapter entitled "A Global Dialogue on Federalism: Conceptual Framework" in the corresponding theme book[1].

The Global Dialogue program explores federalism by theme. Examples of future themes include the distribution of powers, legislative and executive governance, fiscal federalism, and foreign relations. Each theme is led by a "theme coordinator" who makes use of the most current research on the theme to create an internationally comprehensive set of questions covering institutional provisions and how they work in practice. This set of questions, or "theme template," is the foundation of the program, as it guides the dialogue at the roundtables and forms the outline for the theme book. The theme coordinator also selects a representative sample of federal countries and recommends a coordinator for each featured country. Each country coordinator organizes a roundtable, participates in the international

---

1 *Constitutional Origins, Structure, and Change in Federal Countries.* John Kincaid and G. Alan Tarr, eds. (Montreal & Kingston: McGill-Queen's University Press, 2005).

roundtable, and writes a country article for the booklet and a chapter for the book.

As mentioned above, in each featured country, the country coordinator organizes a full-day roundtable event guided by the theme template. The template is distributed to all program participants, allowing equal access to the most current and relevant research. In order to develop the most accurate picture of the theme in their country, it is essential that those participating in the roundtable are representative of the diverse viewpoints in the country, include both practitioners and academics, and are open to sharing with and learning from others. Upon arrival at the roundtable, participants agree on the most important template questions for their dialogue, and spend most of the day exploring those questions, finishing by considering new insights. The country roundtable has been described as a unique opportunity for experts from diverse academic and governmental areas of knowledge and practice to exchange their views on common issues in a neutral environment. As one Belgian participant noted, "All of the participants were particularly impressed by the format: a select group of 20 people who are directly involved in the issue and primed for a constructive exchange, using a backdrop of already-prepared questions. The group included various practicing experts in the area, academics from different institutions, and Flemish and Francophone, who rarely have the occasion to have a dialogue as we did, with much frankness and conviviality."

After each country has held a roundtable, coordinators and roundtable representatives gather at an international roundtable to discuss the key questions that emerged from their roundtables. Those attending share knowledge gained from their own roundtables and identify patterns and differences while seeking new insights. The diversity of the countries and viewpoints offer participants a broad understanding of the theme for a truly comparative dialogue.

The reflections and new insights from the roundtables form the basis of both the booklet and book series. In keeping with its more limited scope and the intent to share the insights gained within a short time frame, the booklet is published soon after the international roundtable. It is widely distributed to a broad audience and is available in several languages, including English, French, and Spanish. The book series provides far more detailed information about each country as well as a chapter summarizing comparative conclusions. The Global Dialogue's publications are intended to fill many gaps in the literature on comparative federalism and provide a rich foundation of knowledge.

The program also includes a website that provides on-line access to a discussion forum, which enables people around the world to become involved in the Global Dialogue. All Global Dialogue articles and chapters are also available on-line at www.forumfed.org.

Readers of this booklet are encouraged to use the knowledge gained to inspire new solutions, thereby strengthening democratic governance, and to join the many Global Dialogue participants around the world to expand and strengthen the growing international network on federalism.

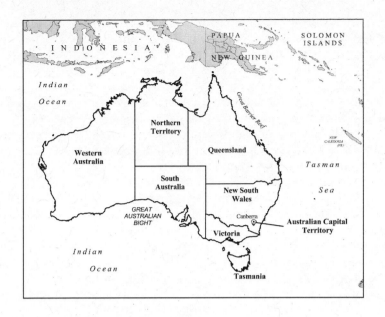

Australia:
The Evolution of a Constitution

KATY LE ROY AND CHERYL SAUNDERS

The Australian federal Constitution has lasted for over 100 years, but
has proved capable of adapting to changing circumstances nevertheless. The text of the Constitution has changed little since 1901, with
only 8 of 44 referendums for change having been successful. Gradual
evolution in the meaning and operation of the text has taken place,
however, through judicial interpretation and changing political practice. One of the major evolutionary changes has been the gradual expansion of the powers of the Commonwealth, or federal, government
and Parliament. Although the system of government created by the
Constitution remains stable, there are current arguments for constitutional change to protect rights more effectively and to establish Australia as a republic.

Australia's Constitution was negotiated during the last decade of the
nineteenth century and came into force on the first of January, 1901.
It was not the product of upheaval, but rather the result of a desire for
limited union for a range of practical reasons on the part of the six colonies that became the Australian states. The Constitution combines

United States-style federalism with British institutions of parliamentary responsible government whereby the prime minister is selected from amongst the members of Parliament. The polity comprises six states, two self-governing mainland territories, and some external territories.

Although the Constitution was originally enacted by the British Parliament, Australia gradually achieved independence from Britain without any formal constitutional change or break in legal continuity. Australia's Constitution was also approved through a relatively popular process of referendums in all six colonies. It is quite a brief document, comprising 127 sections and 11,908 words.

The two primary aims of the Constitution were to establish a federation and to provide for the institutions of national government. These aims were satisfactorily achieved, although the brevity of the Constitution makes it misleading in some respects about the way in which Australian government actually works. The Constitution builds upon and assumes the pre-existing common law. Many important rules of a constitutional character lie outside the formal Constitution.

The text of the Australian Constitution has proved difficult to change. A bill to alter the Constitution that has been passed by the Parliament must be approved in a referendum before it becomes law. Approval in a referendum requires the support of a majority of voters nationally and a majority of voters in a majority of states. As noted above, only 8 of 44 proposals for change have succeeded. Possible reasons for this record are the highly adversarial character of the referendum process, lack of understanding of proposals for change, and the conservatism of Australian voters on constitutional issues. Constitutional issues attract relatively little interest in Australia. Typically, Australians claim to know very little about the Constitution. Public education is complicated by the fact that the text of the Constitution does not deal with some of the institutions of government with which people are most familiar, including the Cabinet and the office of Prime Minister.

In the final decade of the twentieth century, the main subject of constitutional debate in Australia was whether to break Australia's formal links with the Crown and establish a republic, and the form such a republic might take. The 1999 referendum on this question failed largely because of the perceived deficiencies of the alternative arrangements that would have been put in place. It is likely that the question of whether to establish a republic will continue to be a dominant constitutional issue in the early part of the current century, not because it causes particular practical difficulty, but for symbolic reasons.

Neither the Commonwealth nor the state constitutions include a bill or charter of rights. The Constitution provides no express protection for individual rights, although a handful of limits on Commonwealth power have a similar effect. At the time the Constitution was written, countries within the British constitutional tradition were satisfied that rights could be protected adequately by other means. Unlike other comparable countries, now including the United Kingdom itself, Australia has continued to adhere to this view. Successive attempts to introduce a national bill of rights have failed. Consistent with this somewhat complacent view of the ordinary legal system's capacity adequately to protect rights, there has been no general incorporation into Australian law of international human rights instruments to which Australia is a party. Australian law is assumed to be in compliance with them. Corrective action is possible, although not always forthcoming, if, as sometimes happens, this assumption is shown to be misplaced.

Australia is now the only country in the common law world that has no systematic rights protection. It seems likely that rights will be the subject of constitutional debate at some stage in the future. A legislative bill of rights, enacted by the Commonwealth Parliament, using its power to make laws about "external affairs" would offer less of a challenge to the elected institutions of national government and may be preferred to a constitutional bill for that reason. On the other hand, Commonwealth legislation of this kind would override inconsistent state law and would attract state opposition for that reason. In the face of these difficulties, for the foreseeable future, rights protection in Australia is likely to be left to the traditional mechanisms of the Parliament and the courts, developing the single Australian common law.

In some respects, the Constitution has been remarkably successful. It brought and has peacefully kept together all parts of a geographically very large country, resisting at least one serious attempt at secession. It has functioned as the principal constituent instrument during more than a century of stable democratic government. It has been flexible enough to adapt to dramatically changing circumstances, including transition to Australian independence. It has provided a framework of government within the limits of which Commonwealth, state, and territory communities have developed and flourished. However, partly because of its longevity, the Constitution has become increasingly irrelevant to the structure and operation of Australian government, at least for those who regard the purpose of constitutions as being to structure power and control its abuse. More change to the Constitution is probably necessary, and will require increased public education about the constitutional system, a robust public debate, and some attitudinal change.

> Partly because of its longevity, the Constitution has become increasingly irrelevant to the structure and operation of Australian government

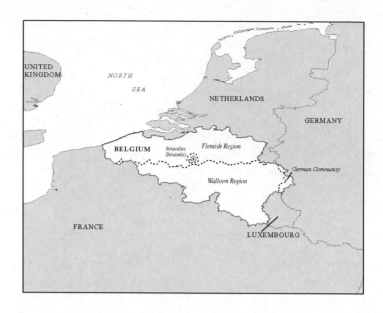

Belgium:
Ambiguity and Disagreement

KRIS DESCHOUWER

Belgium became a federal country gradually, starting in the 1970s and culminating in the early 1990s. The motive for federalism was to manage tensions between the Dutch-speaking north of the country and the French-speaking south. Interestingly, the north and the south still have somewhat different visions of their federal system. This disagreement has made its way into the Constitution. North and south also still disagree on the very definition of language rights and minority groups, a principal reason why these are not clearly defined in the Constitution. Ongoing ambiguity and deep disagreement are basic ingredients of a federal structure that – surprisingly enough – continues to function quite effectively, without major conflicts.

Belgium's federal system officially came into being in 1993 following piecemeal reforms meant to accommodate ethno-linguistic differences. As such, the framers of the Belgian Constitution did not find their inspiration in existing models of federal countries. The Belgian federation did not result from the implementation of a blueprint; nor did anyone invent or imagine the new Belgium. Rather, it is the product of a series of subtle compromises between two divergent views of how the old unitary state had to be reformed.

Probably the most striking feature of the Belgian federation is its dual nature. Belgium is a federation of language communities and also of territorial regions. This double federation is the result of conflicting views between Dutch speakers and French speakers on the ideal configuration of the country. The first demands for devolution came from the Dutch speakers and were based on the defence of their language. The Dutch speakers wanted autonomy granted to the two major language communities. Brussels – situated north of the linguistic borderline – would have been incorporated into, or at least intimately linked to, the Dutch-speaking, or Flemish, community. Alternately, the Francophones defended granting autonomy to regions, which meant that Brussels, with a population that was 85 percent Francophone, would have become a region in the Belgian federation rather than being part of the Flemish community.

A complex double federation provided a way out of this deadlock. Belgium created both the language communities suggested by the Dutch-speakers and the territorial regions preferred by the Francophones. The three regions are Francophone Wallonia, bilingual Brussels, and Dutch-speaking Flanders. The Dutch-speaking community can exercise its powers in the Flemish region and in Brussels, and the French-speaking community can exercise its powers in the Walloon region and in Brussels. This arrangement is certainly much more complicated than that of other federations, which are simply divided into territorially defined sub-states. But it has the major advantage of offering a solution to two diverging, and to a large extent incompatible, views on the very nature of the country. The Belgian federal Constitution thus accepts and defines two visions of the country and allows them to coexist.

> The Belgian federal Constitution thus accepts and defines two visions of the country and allows them to coexist.

Yet this coexistence is not without its problems. The city of Brussels is now a region, but one whose Dutch-speaking minority needs to be protected. The Dutch speakers have a number of reserved seats in the regional parliament and half of the ministers in the executive of the region.

The creation of a Flemish region in the north of the country has also left some 60,000 Francophones on the 'wrong side of the border'. The Francophones of Flanders therefore need to be protected. The practical solution for these French speakers has been to create an exception for the communities in which they live called "communes à facilités." The Francophones who live in those communities can use French to communicate with the regional and federal public authorities.

However, controversy has emerged over the definition, interpretation, and extent of these French language rights within Flemish territory. Among many Dutch speakers, the limited French language services are seen as a temporary exception to the principle of territoriality, a means of accommodating the linguistic minorities until they learn the language of the region sufficiently to communicate with public authorities. Although the minority rights in these designated zones have been entrenched in the Constitution, Flanders regularly demands their removal because they are an exception to the rule of territorially-based language. The Dutch speakers argue that the relation between the language groups has been settled by the federal organization of the Belgian state.

Among Francophones, opinion on the language rights question is decidedly different. They regard the French speakers in Flanders as a minority in need of the same formal protection that the very small Dutch-speaking minority in Brussels has received. They reject the notion that the rights of these French speakers in Flanders should be seen as a transitional measure. On the contrary, they consider them to be fundamental and further argue that these rights should not be limited to only a small number of "communes à facilités." For instance, in certain municipalities with significant Francophone minorities French speakers have no protection at all. This includes the Francophones living in the major Flemish cities of Antwerp and Ghent.

Belgium's Francophones refer to international law – particularly the Council of Europe's Framework Convention for the Protection of National Minorities – in demanding better protection in general for the Francophones in Flanders. They define the French speakers of Flanders as a minority that deserves proper cultural protection, whereas the Dutch speakers argue that linguistic rights should be based on a clear link between territory and the use of language. In short, the Dutch speakers do not agree that explicit linguistic or cultural rights should be given to minority groups living in the Dutch-speaking part of the country.

This debate is typical of the public discourse that has been ongoing for decades in Belgium. Until the 1980s these disputes and the ensuing controversy caused the early demise of quite a number of Belgian governments. It is a testament to the current model that it has been able to withstand a high degree of difference of opinion and ambiguity.

Brazil: The Challenges of Constitutional Implementation

CELINA SOUZA

With seven different constitutions in its 115 years of federal governance, Brazil is now under the aegis of the 1988 Constitution. It is a result of the country's return to democracy after almost 20 years under a military regime. Brazil has had a variety of federal arrangements and has experienced periods of authoritarianism and democracy. The country's main social conundrums, regional and social inequality and poverty, while of concern to constitution makers since the 1930s, have not been vigorously addressed by any political system.

Federalism was introduced in 1889 and laid out in the 1891 Constitution. Unlike in many federal polities, federalism in Brazil was never a response to deep social fissures along ethnic, linguistic, and religious lines. Because the unity of the country has not been an issue since Brazil became a federal republic, the Constitution states that "all power emanates from the people," not from the nation as a community with a common history, from the state as organized under one government, or from the constituent units as member states of the federation, signalling that Brazil's federal system is built on the principle of individualism rather than communalism.

The 1988 Constitution expresses a constitutional tradition developed throughout the writing of seven constitutions. What distinguishes the 1988 Constitution is the popular participation that went into its creation. This was a vital element of the transition to democracy and became an important instrument for the legitimization of the Constitution and re-democratization overall. The Constitution's main political and policy objectives were to create a just society, to guarantee national development, to eradicate poverty and marginalization, to reduce social and regional inequalities, and to promote the well-being of all people without prejudice and discrimination. It provides the basic principles, rules, and rights, but also a wide range of public policies. It also (a) institutes municipalities as a tier of governance in addition to the states; (b) provides more resources to constituent units, in particular to local governments; (c) expands societal and institutional control over the three orders of government by increasing the power of both the legislature and the judiciary and by recognizing the role of social movements and of non-governmental institutions in controlling the government; and (d) universalizes social services, in particular access to health care.

> The main problems Brazil faces today are due more to governmental difficulties in changing policy priorities ... than to deficiencies in the Constitution itself.

Why then has Brazil had difficulties maintaining a stable federal democracy – one that is capable of preventing periods of authoritarian rule, reducing social and regional inequality and poverty, and reconciling social democracy with the constraints of the world economy? The main problems Brazil faces today are due more to governmental difficulties in changing policy priorities and dealing with economic constraints not foreseen by constitution makers than to deficiencies in the Constitution itself. There is a gap between the areas constitutional governance explicitly covers and politico-economic circumstances, and the latter still continue to take precedence over constitutional mandates.

The specific problems currently facing Brazil's federalism and constitutional governance involve several issues. First and most importantly, Brazil is a federation that has always been characterized by regional and social inequality. Although the 1988 Constitution and those preceding it have provided several political and fiscal mechanisms for offsetting regional inequality and tackling poverty, these mechanisms have not been able to overcome the historical differences among regions and social classes.

Governments of the three orders have not been able to reduce poverty and regional inequality. Their ability to act is limited by a number of factors, not the least of which is the fiscal requirements of international lenders and federal financial institutions and regulations. The states' capacity is also limited by their debt payments.

Another factor adversely affecting states is the opening up of Brazil's economy. This tends to make intergovernmental relations more complex, as it increases the differences between developed and less developed states. This also contributes to the current trend toward reversing previous, although timid, initiatives favouring economic decentralization.

An added issue is that in Brazil there are few mechanisms to provide for coordination between the three orders of government. This has become more important because municipal governments have had their financial standing upgraded within the federation vis-à-vis the states and have also been given responsibility for important social policies.

The prospect of transforming constitutional principles into policies for regional development is not currently on the agenda for Brazil. But transformation is not impossible given that overcoming regional inequality has always been a priority of Brazil's constitution makers. As well, it is not impossible to foresee greater clarification of the role of the states in the federation. This is because the states' debts and problems, including their failure to fight violence and drug trafficking, are now a high priority for the country as a whole.

Finally, there is now consensus that an in-depth review of fiscal and taxation mechanisms and of the role of each order of government in the federation is necessary. Enough short-term measures have been taken to alert decision makers that significant changes are needed. These changes, however, are likely to be preceded by broad debate involving governmental and private interests.

How the resolution of significant conflicts of interest is likely to be negotiated is not yet clear. One thing is almost certain: changes in sensitive areas of interest are likely to create uncertainty among the electorate and investors.

Resolving Brazil's main problems, in particular social and regional inequality depends less on federalism and on the Constitution itself than on addressing broader political conflicts, redefining policy priorities, and improving economic performance. Nevertheless, the use of public policies to overcome a long history of inequality require governmental intervention and resources at a time when many see governments more as a hindrance than as a solution. This view would limit the role of governments, particularly in the developing world, to achieving budget surpluses, much to the detriment of increased public spending.

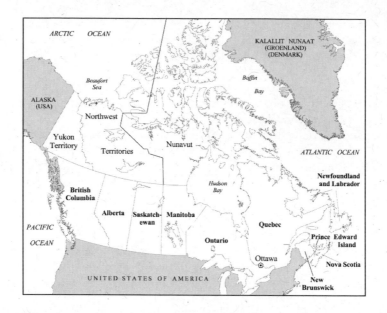

Constitutional Politics in Canada

RAINER KNOPFF AND
ANTHONY SAYERS

Although Canada is one of the world's oldest federal democracies, it is beset by cultural tensions that have recently threatened its disintegration. Credible separatist challenges from the province of Quebec, Canada's predominantly French-speaking jurisdiction, began in the mid-1970s and culminated in a 1995 Quebec referendum that came within a whisker (1.2%) of approving secession.

Quebec claims the status of a "distinct society" on the grounds that it represents one of Canada's two founding nations, meaning that the other nine provinces are subdivisions of the English-speaking nation. The other provinces advance a vision of equal provincial status instead. The result is a decentralizing dynamic.

The territorial version of "two nations" (i.e., Quebec and the rest of Canada) competes with the idea of a bilingual Canada in which individuals of either linguistic group can be equally at home throughout the country. Both interpretations of the French and English duality are in turn challenged by the idea of a multicultural Canada. At the same time, Canada's indigenous peoples have redefined themselves as "First Nations" entitled to self-government, perhaps even becoming a constitutional third order of government. Not to be outdone, Canada's increasingly vociferous municipalities are demanding similar "third order" status. For their part, Canada's three northern territories sometimes covet provincial status. Canadian women have built on the symbolism of "founding" or "first" nations by underlining the salience of "founding genders." Added to this volatile brew is a strand of individual, rights-based politics set against the politics of group identity.

Governing this diverse and sparsely populated country are federal and provincial parliaments exhibiting highly disciplined parties, dominated by their first ministers, and elected by plurality vote in single member constituencies. Because the effectiveness and influence of government members from less populous regions are difficult to discern under conditions of party discipline, opposition parties often attract regional protest votes. The electoral system further regionalizes parties by magnifying the impact of regionally concentrated votes, so that a party's share of seats in a particular region is often much higher or lower than its proportion of the regional vote. Electoral reform is thus a part of Canada's ongoing institutional debate.

So is parliamentary reform. Reducing party discipline in the House of Commons is a prominent proposal; reforming the federal Senate is another. Reformers want to make the Senate a more effective check on the House of Commons by transforming it from an appointed to an elected body with a more equal representation of the provinces.

From the 1960s through the 1990s this panoply of issues generated a growing wave of constitutional reform proposals. Beginning as an attempt to resolve the challenges posed by Quebec nationalism and separatism, the process grew into one of so-called mega-constitutional politics, in which all of the conflicting interests and visions came to be reflected in ever more unwieldy proposals of omnibus constitutional transformation.

Out of the process of mega-constitutional politics came the Constitution Act, 1982, which added two important elements to the original 1867 Constitution: 1) a fully domestic amending procedure, overcoming the need to have major amendments enacted by the British Parliament, and 2) a judicially enforceable Charter of Rights and Freedoms. The Charter was intended not just to protect rights and freedoms but also to provide a counterweight to the federal constitution's emphasis on territorial division by constitutionalizing values Canadians held in common.

The Constitution Act, 1982 did not, however, satisfy all voices in the raucous chorus of constitutional demands. Indeed, because it limited Quebec's assumed right to a constitutional veto, it entrenched individual rather than territorial bilingualism, and failed to decentralize federal powers. Quebec saw 1982 as a slap in the face, and was the only province to reject the 1982 reform.

Two subsequent rounds of major constitutional reform were launched – the Meech Lake (1987) and Charlottetown (1992) rounds. Meech Lake was motivated by the attempt to "bring Quebec back into the Canadian constitutional family," but the effort engendered demands to deal, not only with Quebec's priorities for constitutional reform, but those of native peoples, women, minority groups, and other provinces. The subsequent process, which addressed all of the major demands for recognition and constitutional change, produced the Charlottetown Accord, which, when put to a referendum, failed to gain majority approval.

Included in the failed Meech Lake and Charlottetown accords were provisions to constitutionally recognize Quebec as a "distinct society" within Canada. Failure to achieve this reform contributed to the near success of the 1995 Quebec secession referendum. Secessionist flames then subsided, however, and constitutional fatigue has discouraged further adventures of the mega-constitutional sort.

> The country now appears to have a very full and vibrant slate of institutional reform without the sense of impending demise.

Institutional reform has by no means fallen off the table, however. The focus has simply shifted from formal constitutional amendments – and especially complex packages of such amendments – to more piecemeal changes through parliamentary resolutions, legislation, negotiation, and judicial interpretation. Some of what was demanded during the Meech and Charlottetown episodes – e.g., recognition of Quebec as a distinct society, a *de facto* veto for Quebec over certain constitutional amendments, the progress of First Nations self-government agreements – has been achieved through these mechanisms. Some provinces have instituted a fixed-term election cycle, thus weakening one of the sources of first ministerial power, and are exploring systems of proportional representation.

The fact that these and other reform proposals occur singly and at the sub-constitutional order, rather than being bundled into mega-constitutional packages, appears to have lowered the temperature of institutional politics. Canada has come close to constitutional crisis in recent years. The country now appears to have a very full and vibrant slate of institutional reform without the sense of impending demise. There are no guarantees in politics, but Canada's status as one of the world's oldest and most successful federal democracies may endure for some time.

Germany: Overlapping Powers and Political Entanglements

JUTTA KRAMER

The Federal Republic of Germany was founded in 1949, four years after Germany's defeat in World War II, after the Western Allies gave the prime ministers of the constituent states, or *Länder*, the task of drafting a new constitution with a federal character. Their goal was to prevent a strong central state from arising in Germany again. The resulting federal system is characterized by interconnections and overlapping powers between the central government and the constituent units.

Current challenges to Germany's federal structure include whether or not the system as it stands provides for an adequate constitutional relationship between the federation and the states; whether or not it sufficiently fulfils democratic requirements; and most importantly at present, whether or not the system is capable not only of carrying, but also of surviving the burdens of German unification with its political, economic, and constitutional consequences.

The constitution of the Federal Republic of Germany, called the Basic Law, was drafted and passed by the Parliamentary Council in 1948 and 1949. The Basic Law re-established a federal system and distinguished between three different types of public authorities: the federation, the states, and the Federal Republic of Germany as a whole. In connection with the conundrum of whether or not a successor to the international treaties and obligations of the former German empire existed and who it might have been, the Federal Constitutional Court stated that there was no common frame for such a single successor known as the "Federal Republic of Germany," but only two entities: the federation and the states. When the court made this decision, the ongoing debate on the nature of the German federal system came to an end. Like the majority of federations, Germany consists of a two-order regime.

Despite the dual character of the German federal system, the constitutional relations among and between these two orders form a triplet: namely, relations within the federation, between the federation and states, and inter-state relations. Consequently, the federation as well as each single constituent state has its own constitutional jurisdiction, exercised internally as the constitution-making power. Externally, each has the power to establish and maintain intergovernmental relations with the federation and the constituent states. The only mechanism of cohesion of the three constitutional dimensions is the so called "homogeneity clause" which directs the constitutional order in the *Länder* to conform to the principles of the democratic and social state and the rule of law as defined in the Basic Law. Apart from that one clause, the three constitutional areas co-exist completely separately from one another.

As in any genuine federal form of government, there is not one single working relationship between the federation and the states in the German system, but a multi-faceted network of such relationships, both formal and informal, bilateral and multilateral, individual and collective. The Federal Council, or *Bundesrat,* as Germany's second house of the federation, is at the centre of the federal structure in Germany. In constitutional terms and in working practice, it is the legislative organ representing the states within a federal framework and it also participates in federal administration. The immediate level of coordination is that of horizontal cooperation among the states themselves on the basis of intergovernmental relations.

In this three-dimensional constitutional framework the federation has primacy over the constituent states, as is reflected in its title as the "upper state". It is also responsible for protecting and preserving the federal constitution. Nevertheless the constituent states are "states" in the full meaning of the word, enjoying their own original constitutional power, exercising independently their own functions and competencies, and administering their tasks as an inherent constitution-based domain. Therefore, except as otherwise provided or permitted by the Basic Law, the relationships between the federation and the states, as well as between the states, are governed by the principles of parity and equality. Every state – in spite of its size, number of inhabitants, economic strength, and financial capacity – has an equal federal status under the constitution.

The federal systems in Germany and in the United States both show a clear tendency to uniformity and centralization. But there are three undeniable differences. First, in Germany the development of unitary federalism was driven by the most powerful political organs of the federal government, the popularly-elected first chamber, the *Bundestag*, and the second chamber, the *Bundesrat.* They have granted themselves concurrent legislative competencies by amending the constitution when they have had the required two-thirds majority of both houses. Second, in political reality the most effective division of powers is practised by the two different administrations at the federal as well as the state level, thus displaying aspects of executive federalism. That means in practise that the federal government has acquired the largest share of concurrent competencies as the main legislator in Germany, while the *Länder* as the executors not only of their own laws, but also of the bulk of the federal legislation, function essentially as administrative bodies. Third, with joint tasks and joint taxes belonging to both the federal and the state governments, there is a great deal of overlapping powers, political entanglements, and consensus-seeking procedures – a characteristic of cooperative federalism.

However, the system of cooperative federalism has proved to be not only crippling on a practical level, but also problematic from a democratic point of view. If everyone is made to be responsible for everything, the result is that nobody becomes responsible for anything. For this reason, there has been much discussion about instituting reforms to produce greater transparency with regard to decision making and responsibility, and about permitting more competition between the federal government and the *Länder*. However, Germany is still far from having a system of competitive federalism.

> The system of cooperative federalism has proved to be not only crippling on a practical level, but also problematic from a democratic point of view.

After 45 years of the East-West political division of Germany due to Cold War conflict, the reunification of Germany took place in 1990. The German Democratic Republic (GDR) joined the territory covered by the Basic Law *(Grundgesetz)* after the GDR collapsed-politically and economically. In the process of reunification, the country decided that in order to restore previous states as the basis for any implementation of a federal system, one should for the time being return to the traditional structures in East Germany, creating "the new *Länder*", while leaving the reform of the federal structure to a later date. It seems certain that the federation will have to offer massive subsidies for quite some time to the newly incorporated East German states. While this problem has long been recognized, it nevertheless poses a considerable threat to the development of the federal system in the next few years. This situation could introduce a prolonged period of centralization in German federalism such as happened in the years following the foundation of the Federal Republic until the financial reforms of 1966 to 1969.

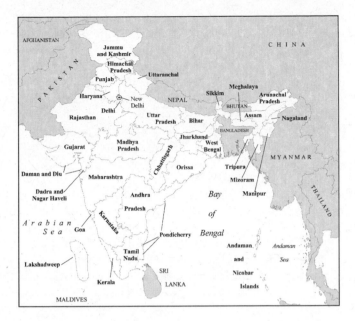

India:
The Emergence of Cooperative Federalism

AKHTAR MAJEED

The Constitution of India envisaged a creative balance between the need for an effective Centre and empowered states. The federal system that emerged became the sound framework for the working of the Indian state. In spite of the difficulty of maintaining a balance of powers, the system has survived.

A country the size of a continent, with an area of 12,650 000 sq. miles and a population of over a billion, India is a diverse society with 18 national languages and some 2000 dialects, a dozen ethnic and seven religious groups fragmented into a large number of sects, castes, and sub-castes, and some sixty socio-cultural sub-regions spread over seven natural geographic regions. Before independence in 1947, India had been under the jurisdiction of first the British East India Company and then the British Crown for the preceding two centuries.

From 1946 to 1950, the leaders of India's Freedom Movement and the founding fathers of the Constitution had the task of drafting the

Constitution. The members of this Constituent Assembly shared two main goals. The first was to build a united polity out of a highly fragmented and segmented society, which they attempted through strengthening the "Union" or federal order, by shifting residuary powers to it. Their second aim was to develop a highly undeveloped country by reducing poverty and illiteracy and building a modern nation state. The result was to be the longest constitution in the world with 395 Articles, 12 schedules, and 3 appendices.

The Constitution establishes a "Union of States," which now consists of 28 states, six "Union Territories," and one National Capital Territory. It also defines the powers of the executive, legislative, and judicial branches of government; provides a standard by which the validity of the laws enacted by the legislature is tested; and establishes the judiciary as the guardian of the Constitution. The Constitution is generally flexible but rigid in many of its "federal" matters that pertain to the states. Consequently, the Constitution, reflecting concerns about centrifugal forces that might fragment India, establishes a rather centralized polity in which the Union government is vested with sufficient powers to ensure not only its dominance, but also its ability to rule in a unitary fashion if necessary and politically feasible.

Equally important, the country's diversity and socio-economic conditions, coupled with the ideological influences of socialism, drove the Constitution toward a more unitary federalism in the name of justice, equality, and rights protection. Only a strong Centre, thought many of the founders, could effectively drive economic development and ensure equity across territorial jurisdictions, religions, languages, classes, and castes. Hence the trend generally was toward ever more centralization under the Congress Party from independence to the 1980s. During the 1980s, however, Union-state relations became more rancorous, the Congress party began to decline, and a coalition government, the National Front, assumed power in New Delhi as a result of the 1989 elections-in part because centralized federalism driven by a monopoly party for some 40 years had fallen far short of achieving the objectives set forth in the Constitution. Since 1989, coalition governments at the Centre, proliferating regional and state parties across the country, and liberalization of the economy have served to decentralize the federal political system in many respects.

However, despite decentralization in some areas, there is still widespread opinion that the mechanisms of inter-governmental relations in

> Only a strong Centre, thought many of the founders, could effectively drive economic development and ensure equity across territorial jurisdictions, religions, languages, classes, and castes.

India are tilted in favour of the central government. The strong Centre that the founders envisaged has created its own set of problems.

Article 356, or "President's Rule," in which a state's assembly can be dissolved or suspended at the behest of the central government for its "unconstitutional" behaviour, has become one of the most hotly debated topics of the Indian Constitution. Article 356 was introduced for emergencies in which a state government fails to behave in accordance with the provisions of the Constitution. However, the sole judge of that behaviour has been the central government. Often considered to have been used indiscriminately in the past, steps are being taken now to safeguard against future abuses.

Another illustration of potential over-centralization is an imbalance between the powers of taxation assigned to the Union and the states in light of the social-economic responsibilities assigned to each. The Constitution regulates in elaborate detail the legislative and administrative relations between the Union and states, and the distribution of revenues between them. The Union has been invested with a larger field for the operation of its legislative and executive authority than is to be found in most other federal constitutions.

A similar imbalance of revenue and responsibilities exists between the state and municipal orders as does between the Union and the states. While, the Constitution confers constitutional status on the municipal order, their 'autonomous' functioning has yet to be established. Known as "Panchayats" in rural areas, the municipal bodies do not possess the financial backing or necessary expertise to maximize their authority. However, one positive outcome of the municipal order is that, due to the Constitution reserving a certain number of seats for women and specified castes and tribes, these traditionally disadvantaged groups have been able to gain experience. They are then enabled to work toward participation at the state or national orders.

The Indian Constitution would seem to create a cooperative Union of states rather than a dual polity. Planning for mobilisation of national resources and their most effective and balanced utilisation for the social and economic development of the country as a whole now appears to be an integral part of this concept. Through allocation of financial resources and centralized planning, the Union has extended its role into areas which used to lie exclusively within the states' domain. On the other hand, redistribution of responsibilities through devolution of powers from the Union to the states and from the states to the Panchayats is facilitating the attainment of the objectives of the Constitution: unity, social justice, and democracy. All this indicates steps in the direction of cooperative federalism.

Mexican Federalism in
the Democratic Transition

JUAN MARCOS GUTIÉRREZ GONZÁLEZ

During the twentieth century, the story of Mexican federalism was mostly one of centralization, which has only been countered since about 1982 by demands and policies for governmental decentralization, political democratization, and economic liberalization. The provisions of the current constitution, the Constitution of 1917, clearly reflect major issues and concerns prevalent in Mexico in the past that are still with us in the present. Among some of these issues are the overriding power of the president, decentralization, and the establishment of a truly federal system. Today, Mexico is struggling to define its own version of federalism and to put an end to the centripetal force that has dominated national life.

Mexico has a long tradition of centralism extending back through the colonial era and into the Aztec and Mayan civilizations. In the creation of Mexico's first federal constitution in 1824, while the framers did not possess any overriding vision of the federation, they knew what they hoped to avoid. Among the reasons for creating the Constitution and adopting a federal regime was the intention of abolishing absolutism through the foundation of a system of weights and counterweights between the government and the people, as well as granting the states a representative government

> Mexico has a long tradition of centralism extending back through the colonial era and into the Aztec and Mayan civilizations.

Even though Mexico's current constitution is relatively young, its federal principles stem directly from the first federal constitution that came into effect in 1824. From 1836 to 1854, however, Mexico had a centralist constitution, but experiences under this constitution triggered a resurgence of federalist ideas, which culminated in the federal Constitution of 1857. This constitution, which failed to stem centralization, remained in effect until the outcome of the Mexican Revolution led to the 1917 Constitution that is in effect today.

The victors of the Mexican Revolution had some clear federalist and democratic objectives, in part because the Revolution began as a rebellion in several states against the centralized, dictatorial regime of Porfirio Díaz. Under the federal model framed in the Constitution, however, the legislative and judicial branches of the federal government have been essentially subservient to the overarching power of the executive. From 1920 to 1995, the federal system was characterized by a constitutional centralization of powers in the hands of the federal government, which considerably diminished the decision-making powers of the states and municipalities. This system brought about a sociopolitical phenomenon that characterized Mexico's political life during the twentieth century: the powerful presidential system.

In addition, a single political party, the *Partido Revolucionario Institucional* (PRI – Institutional Revolutionary Party), maintained nearly monopolistic control over the country's political life. From its founding in 1929 until 1989, the PRI controlled the presidency, the Congress of the Union, the 31 state governments, the Federal District, and most of the nation's 2,448 municipal governments. The PRI lost the presidency for the first time only in 2000, after opposition parties had already gained control of a number of state and municipal governments.

Currently, political events never seen before in Mexico have arrived with the growing development of associations of municipalities, and the so called National Conference of Governors (CONAGO) which foster and demand the recovering of the political and financial autonomy lost during seven decades. The main agenda of these associations and the National Conference of Governors is to address the subject of fiscal federalism. Added to this mix is the increasing activism of legislators from both Chambers of Congress. They have developed various constitutional reform proposals with several focal points but all sharing the intent of reconsidering the federal model. Some suggested changes include limiting, perhaps substantially, the powers of the president of the republic, and strengthening the notion of Mexico as a federal republic by more clearly specifying the three orders of government.

The structure of the Constitution was organized in the division of three powers: executive, legislative, and judiciary and three orders of government: the federal, state, and municipal spheres. While the Constitution established a federal system with substantial powers residing, in principle, in the states, the document also established a highly secular social-welfare state that is largely under the purview of the federal government whose authority to intervene in such matters as foreign and domestic trade, agriculture, food supplies, labour, health care, education, and energy facilitated centralization, and whose ownership of land and natural resources fostered a highly nationalized economy. The Mexican system's features resemble those of cooperative federalism which, in practice, ended up strengthening a great deal the federal sphere to the detriment of the states and municipalities, undermining federalism as such.

Furthermore, in Mexico the distribution of concurrent intergovernmental powers and responsibilities provided in the Constitution is neither clear nor sufficient, and this has generated uncertainty, conflicts, duplicity, and has caused the centralization of great areas of national life. Proponents of change have argued that federal, state, and municipal responsibilities should be redefined and listed in the Constitution.

Another ongoing debate in Mexico is whether or not the Senate should be changed to become truly representative of the states, and whether some or all of its members should be members of the state legislatures.

A final point to consider is that one of the main actions to be taken for federalism to function properly is to grant all orders of government with a real ability to generate the majority of the financial resources that they require. Such a move would undo the current fiscal centralization, which has created an almost total dependence of the states and municipalities on federal transfers.

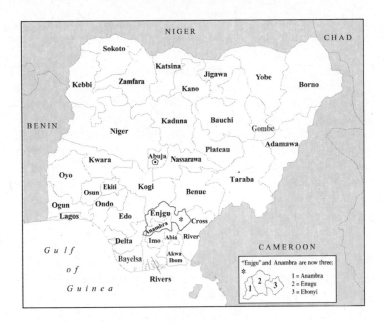

Nigeria:
In Need of Good Governance

IGNATIUS AKAAYAR AYUA

Nigeria came into existence in 1900, in the form of the British Protectorates of Northern and Southern Nigeria and the Colony of Lagos. These units were amalgamated under a single British administration in 1914, and from then until 1954 Nigeria was governed as a unitary state. This is a story familiar to students of European imperialism: a new state – Nigeria – created not by the voluntary union of previously existing, closely related, and freely contracting political units, but imposed by an imperial power on an artificially demarcated territory containing a heterogeneous population of people who up to then had been essentially strangers to each other. In the context of the emergence of the Nigerian federation, the absence of an enabling environment for a credible negotiation of federal-state relations in part accounts for several of Nigeria's current constitutional challenges, including distribution of powers, revenue-sharing, a unitary judiciary, and "indigene" rights.

Although formally governed as a unitary state for forty years, Nigeria was composed of three very distinct administrative regions: the Western

Region, dominated by the Yorubas; the Eastern Region, dominated by the Igbos; and the vast Northern Region, dominated by the Hausa-Fulani ruling class of the famous Sokoto Caliphate of the 19th century. When Nigeria was converted into a federation under the so-called Lyttleton Constitution of 1954, these three regions were the federating units. Britain's final constitutional enactment respecting Nigeria – the Independence Constitution of 1960 – preserved this same federal structure. But since independence the country has been subdivided five times into a total of 36 states and the Federal Capital Territory of Abuja.

Nigeria's post-independence history has been marked by two long periods of military rule – from 1966 to 1979 and again from 1984 to 1999. The country's two principal post-independence constitutions – the 1979 Constitution and the 1999 Constitution – were fathered on the country by military rulers before returning the reins of power to civilians.

The 1979 Constitution made major changes in the way Nigeria was governed. It replaced the cabinet-style of government inherited from the British with a US-style presidential system; instituted local governments as the third order of government; and promoted a robust federal structure in order to reduce ethnic tensions by affirming the differences among Nigeria's ethnic groups. The current constitution, which went into effect on 29 May 1999, was the outcome of a transition process led by the military government of General Abdusalami Abubakar. Except for minor adjustments, the 1999 Constitution is the same as the 1979 Constitution. Surpassing all its postcolonial predecessors, the 1999 Constitution has now been in force for more than five years and has survived its first major test – countrywide general elections conducted in 2003, which resulted in large turnovers in federal and state legislatures and regime changes in many state and local governments.

> Surpassing all its postcolonial predecessors, the 1999 Constitution has now been in force for more than five years and has survived its first major test – countrywide general elections conducted in 2003

Notwithstanding the efforts of the constitution-drafters to entrench federalist structures, the balance of power in Nigeria still favours the central government. Two main factors account for this: long periods of rule by a unified military chain of command, and control by the Centre of the country's main economic resource – oil. The strength of the central government has evoked deep resentment from those who believe that the states are too weak. Many believe that this concentration of power at the Centre is responsible for the large-scale corruption and mismanagement of resources that are now evident in governance. Consequently, there have been calls for further devolution of powers to the constituent units in the federation.

The sharing of the federation's revenue has become a contentious issue. Recently the federal government had to seek constitutional interpretation from the Supreme Court as to the extent the "littoral" states, or states bordering the Gulf of Guinea, could benefit from the offshore oil resources of the country on the principle of derivation. The friction occasioned by the agitation for the control of resources, coupled with the lack of understanding of the flexible mechanism for sharing national resources between the federal government and the other tiers of government, have exacerbated the problem.

Furthermore, the distortion of some established federal principles by the command structure of the military and the need to insulate the judiciary from political interference has led to the evolution of a centralised or unitary judiciary in a federal state. This arrangement, although antithetical to federalism, is largely believed to be the panacea for insulating the judiciary from the monetary pressures and pervasive influence that may have otherwise been exerted on it by state governments.

It is also pertinent to stress that Nigerians have abused the "indigeneship" provisions in the Constitution to the detriment of the enjoyment of citizenship rights in the country. The word "indigene," a Nigerian coinage, is used to define natives of a particular place in relation to more recent citizens of that locality. The adverse effect of the deliberate policy of promoting indigenes, as opposed to "settlers," has been detrimental to efforts to build a strong and united country.

Nigeria's democracy is still fragile and to a large extent crisis ridden. These crises are largely attributable to the poor use of the various consensus building and conflict resolution mechanisms in the Constitution. There is cause for hope that, in spite of the absence of a freely negotiated federal system, the various and disparate ethnic groups in Nigeria have traditionally exhibited harmonizing tendencies among themselves. Even the current political quarrels largely revolve around sharing national resources, using ethnicity and religion as smokescreens.

Nigeria is in dire need of good governance and responsive leadership as successive United Nations' Human Development Index reports have scored Nigeria very low, especially concerning poverty eradication and improvement in the standard of living of the people. The major goal of government should be the evolution of policies and strategies towards reversing this worrisome trend otherwise constitutional governance on any model of federalism, and no matter how ingeniously devised, will be jeopardized.

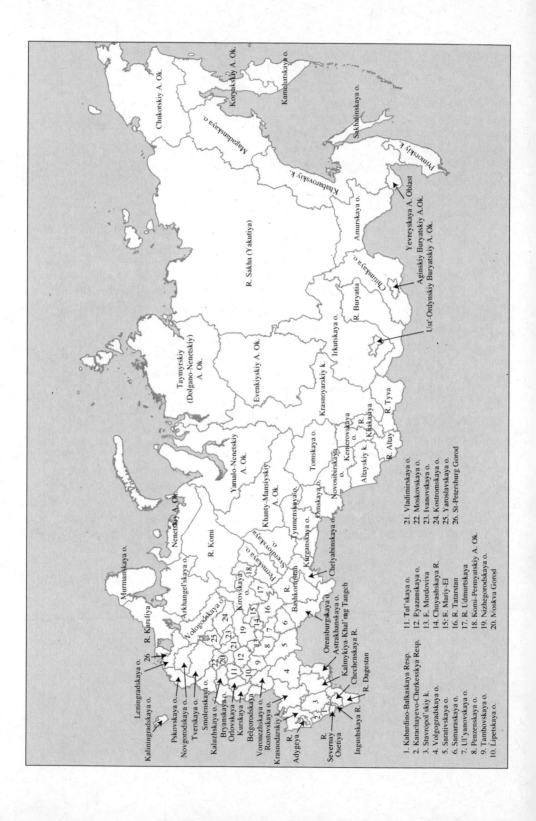

Chukotskiy A. Ok.

Koryakskiy A. Ok.

Kamchatskaya o.

Sakhalinskaya o.

Magadanskaya o.

Primorskiy k.

Khabarovskiy k.

Yevreyskiy A. Oblast
Aginskiy Buryatskiy A.Ok.

R. Sakha (Yakutiya)

Amurskaya o.

Ust'-Ordynskiy Buryatskiy A. Ok.

Chitinskaya o.

R. Buryatia

Irkutskaya o.

Taymyrskiy
(Dolgano-Nenetskiy)
A. Ok.

Evenkiyskiy A. Ok.

Krasnoyarskiy k.

R. Tyva

R. Altay

R. Khakasiya

Kemerovskaya o.

Altayskiy k.

Novosibirskaya o.

Tomskaya o.

Omskaya o.

Yamalo-Nenetskiy
A. Ok.

Khanty-Mansiyskiy
A. Ok.

Tyumenskaya o.

Kurganskaya o.

Chelyabinskaya o.

Sverdlovskaya o.

Murmanskaya o.

Nenetskiy A. Ok.

R. Kareliya

R. Komi

Arkhangel'skaya o.

Kaliningradskaya o.

Leningradskaya o.

Pskovskaya o.

Novgorodskaya o.

Tverskaya o.

Smolenskaya o.

Kaluzhskaya o.

Bryanskaya o.

Orlovskaya

Kurskaya

Belgorodskaya

Voronezhskaya o.

Rostovskaya o.

Krasnodarskiy k.

Adygeya

R. Severnay Osetiya

Ingushskaya R.

Chechenskaya R.

R. Dagestan

Kalmykiya-Khal'mg Tangch

Astrakhanskaya o.

Orenburgskaya o.

Permskaya o.

Bashkortostan

Kirovskaya o.

Vologodskaya o.

1. Kabardino-Balkaskaya Resp.
2. Karachayevo-Cherkesskya Resp.
3. Stavropol'skiy k.
4. Volgogradskaya o.
5. Saratovskaya o.
6. Samarskaya o.
7. Ul'yanovskaya o.
8. Penzenskaya o.
9. Tambovskaya o.
10. Lipetskaya o.

11. Tul'skaya o.
12. Ryazanskaya o.
13. R. Mordoviya
14. Chuvashskaya R.
15: R. Mariy-El
16. R. Tatarstan
17. R. Udmurtiya
18. Komi-Permyatskiy A. Ok.
19. Nizhegorodskaya o.
20. Moskva Gorod

21. Vladimirskaya o.
22. Moskovskaya o.
23. Ivanovskaya o.
24. Kostromskaya o.
25. Yaroslavskaya o.
26. St-Petersburg Gorod

Russia: Federalism in Flux

MARAT SALIKOV

Since the Soviet Union's collapse, Russia has been struggling in its efforts to build a democratic political system, market economy, and true federal structure to replace the strict political and economic controls of its communist period. Russia is not only the world's largest country, but also has one of its most complex federal systems. The Russian Federation consists of 89 constituent units, typically referred to as "subjects of the Federation" that are divided into six different categories: republics, territories, regions, autonomous areas, autonomous regions, and federal cities. Russian federalism combines both ethno-federalism and territorial federalism. The current constitution of the Russian Federation dates from 1993 and federal arrangements remain dynamic.

Federalism in Russia was first formally instituted by the federal Constitution of 1918. The most significant development of the Soviet era was the incorporation of the Russian Socialist Federated Soviet Republic (RSFSR) into the Union of Soviet Socialist Republics (USSR), which was officially proclaimed in 1922. Despite its professed commitment to "socialist federalism," the USSR was very much a unitary state. The USSR was based upon a one-party political system rooted in Marxist-Leninist ideology, with an emphasis on "democratic centralism," a centrally planned economy, and a powerfully repressive state machinery. What was true of the USSR was likewise true of the RSFSR; federalism was more a pretence than a reality.

In the early 1990s, after the USSR's dissolution, the federal Constitution was amended to eliminate the term "autonomous" from the title of the republics, the title RSFSR was replaced by "Russian Federation," and the territories, regions, and federal cities were all recognized as members of the new federation. However, under the three-part Federation Treaty of 1992, signed by federal authorities and by all of the constituent units of the Russian Federation except Chechnya and

Tatarstan, these new members did not enjoy rights equal to those of the republics. Only with the adoption of the 1993 Constitution, Russia's current constitution, were the equal rights of all subjects of the federation recognized.

All constituent units of the federation are recognized as self-governing entities, a shift from the Soviet era when only ethnically based units were recognized as "subjects of the federation." All units are now free to adopt their own constitutions or charters without seeking approval from federal bodies, as had been required during the Soviet era. However, under the federation Constitution's supremacy clause, federal law is given precedence over the subnational constitutions.

> Russia's federal system developed out of a unitary state, and there are still vestiges of the unitary tradition not only in the law, but also in popular consciousness.

As well, the territorial integrity of the subjects of the federation is guaranteed. Their borders cannot be changed without their consent as well as the consent of the Federation Council (one chamber of the bicameral parliament or Federal Assembly). Each constituent unit is represented in the Federation Council and has two representatives, one from its legislature and the other from its executive. If the federal government challenges its authority, a constituent unit can seek protection from the Constitutional Court.

Finally, the constituent units exercise both exclusive powers and concurrent powers. These powers extend even into foreign affairs. Constituent units may enter into international economic agreements with the constituent parts of other countries and, with the consent of the federation, even with foreign nations.

Russia's federal system developed out of a unitary state, and there are still vestiges of the unitary tradition not only in the law, but also in popular consciousness. The historical tendency of Russia's development has been from the over-centralized state of the Russian Empire and the Soviet Union/RSFSR to a decentralized federation, although President Putin's policy on federalism shows signs of a new centralization. In the decade since the adoption of the federation Constitution, Russia has made notable advances in instituting federal democracy, but important challenges remain.

One continuing issue involves the structure of the Russian Federation because the delineation of the current "subjects of the federation" occurred only recently, with the adoption of the 1993 Constitution. Controversy continues over whether Russian federalism will be symmetrical or asymmetrical, whether subjects of the federation will have equal rights and powers, or whether the ethnically based republics should enjoy different status. There are also pressures in some political circles to enlarge the constituent units and reduce their number given that many undeveloped units of the federation are heavily reliant on federal subsidies.

The constitutional division of powers between the federal government and the constituent units also raises concerns, particularly given the implementation of concurrent powers. In theory, the exercise of these powers should involve framework legislation by the federal government coupled with more detailed regulation by constituent units in accordance with local conditions. In practice, however, the general guidelines in federal laws have often become detailed legislation that leave almost no role for regional legislators.

The central government's attempts to harmonize federal-regional relations (strengthening vertical relations) could lead to a highly centralized federalism, although resistance to centralization remains entrenched in certain parts of the federation, such as Bashkortostan, Sakha, Sverdlovsk, and Tatarstan.

The most difficult challenge facing the Russian federal system is the Chechen crisis – a major armed conflict on Russian territory sparked by the Chechen Republic proclaiming itself independent, although the federation Constitution does not provide for secession. This declaration has led to two wars (federal interventions), one from 1994 to 1996 and the other from 1999 to 2000. Even now separatist-minded units continue to fight with federal forces and to mount terrorist attacks. Despite these hostilities, in the spring of 2003 voters in a referendum in Chechnya adopted a republican constitution and laws governing the election of the Parliament and the president of Chechnya. New parliamentary elections are scheduled for spring 2005, and President Putin has expressed his desire to sign a treaty with the newly elected officials of the Chechen Republic in order to mend the division of powers between the federal government and the Chechen Republic.

Despite these problems, the federation Constitution is far superior to its predecessors, and a combination of constitutional amendments and interpretations of the Constitutional Court should serve to alleviate its remaining deficiencies.

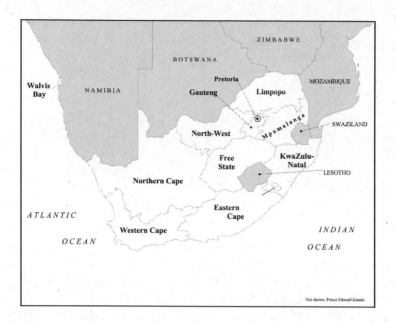

Not shown: Prince Edward Islands

South Africa's Negotiated Compromise

NICO STEYTLER

At the end of three centuries of colonial and racial domination, South Africa adopted a new constitution in 1996 that established a non-racial democracy. The transition from minority rule to majority rule was a "negotiated revolution." The constitution that emerged displays some federal features but nevertheless ensures dominance by the Centre. While nine provinces were established, neither the Constitution nor the political discussions and debates before or after the Constitution used the word "federalism" to apply to South Africa's federal system. With no written reference to itself as a federal country, debate continues on the nature of the new South African state.

The aim of the Constitution was to liberate and empower the oppressed majority in order to rectify past injustices. Coupled with this objective was the desire to unite a country historically divided along racial and ethnic lines. The nation-building enterprise was based on the individualist thrust of human rights that would cut across the old racial divisions, establishing a republic that, according to the preamble of the 1996 Constitution, "belongs to all who live in it, united in our diversity."

The current decentralized system was the product of negotiations – a tug of war between two opposing points of departure: centralism and federalism. The proponents of federalism argued that, given the character of the very centralized pre-1993 government, the new constitution should guarantee that no centralized national government can dictate to the whole country. They argued that a greater dispersal of powers would provide a greater guarantee of democracy. The proponents of centralism – largely represented by the liberation movements – argued that a strong central government was necessary to carry out the important process of transformation. They maintained that the only means to change the conditions of those previously excluded was a strong central government.

South Africa adopted two constitutions in the 1990s – an interim constitution accepted as the result of negotiations in 1993, and a permanent constitution adopted in 1996, two years after the country's first non-racial elections, held in 1994. The federal elements eventually built into the 1993 and 1996 constitutions were the result of the give and take of the negotiation process, and the state that emerged should be seen as a negotiated compromise, not as a product of a single clear vision. Both the interim and the 1996 constitutions articulated two important points of departure from the previous racially-divided democracy. First, the Constitution was based on classical liberal democracy's philosophy of individualism rather than on the protection and entrenchment of groups, be they ethnic, racial, or linguistic. Second, although subnational entities were established, the resulting Constitution avoided a competitive relationship between the subnational entities and the Centre. Nation-building was the overriding concern.

> The federal elements eventually built into the 1993 and 1996 constitutions were the result of the give and take of the negotiation process, and the state that emerged should be seen as a negotiated compromise, not as a product of a single clear vision.

South Africa's Constitution is of interest to other federations for the way power has been dispersed among three spheres of government (national, provincial, and local) and for its explicit articulation of certain principles of cooperative government.

Currently, South Africa has a strong national government and is attempting to develop strong local governments. Yet the Constitution provides a provincial framework indicating that provinces are meant to have a significant role in governance. However, provinces have limited powers of taxation and are dependent on transfers from the Centre for 96 percent of their revenue. Ongoing public debate questions whether the structure of provinces should be strengthened to play a greater role in governance or whether the provincial structure should be watered down.

Before the 1994 democratic elections in South Africa, municipalities were created by statute and organized on a racial basis. While the interim constitution included a chapter on local government, municipalities were placed under the direct control of provinces. The 1996 Constitution fundamentally changed this concept of local government being the lowest tier and instead elevated it to its own sphere alongside those of the national and provincial governments. Furthermore, the 1996 Constitution mandated democratic local governance across the entire country.

A number of factors contributed to this shift in status. Politically, within the liberation movements, local communities played a significant role in the protracted struggle against *apartheid*, giving rise to a strong civic movement. The drafters sought to direct this social movement towards a people-centred development enterprise. The vision of local government as a driver of development also reflected modern development theories wherein local buy-in and initiative are seen as indispensable to social and economic development. Given the fact that the creation of provinces was an uneasy compromise, the strengthening of local government has been at the expense of provinces.

While the sphere of local government is guaranteed a measure of autonomy, there is still a considerable degree of supervision by both the national and provincial governments. Financially, local government has a great measure of autonomy. It has original powers of taxation in the area of property rates and user charges, and currently raises 83 percent of its revenue.

The 1996 Constitution made cooperative government the bedrock of decentralization and has spelled out in broad terms its guiding principles. In the words of the Constitutional Court, the Constitution does not embody "competitive federalism," but, to the contrary, "cooperative government." An important principle of cooperative government is the avoidance of litigation to resolve intergovernmental disputes. The rationale for this principle is that disputes should, where possible, be "resolved at a political level rather than through adversarial litigation." Thus far relations between the Centre and provinces have been cooperative rather than conflictual, much influenced by the dominance of one party in the governance of the provinces and municipalities.

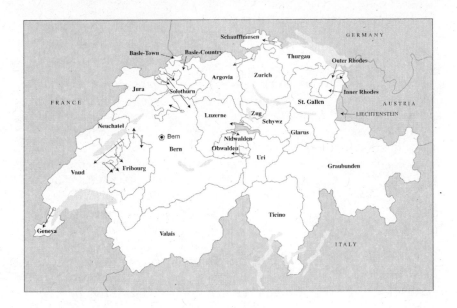

Switzerland:
Crisis of Confidence

NICOLAS SCHMITT

Modern Switzerland's first constitution, dating to 1848, is the second federal constitution of modern times after that of the United States. Its adoption concluded a period of uncertainty during which Switzerland tested a number of governmental systems. The Swiss Constitution has responded well to the needs and expectations of the people. However, some of the reasons for its success – including its highly democratic decision-making process and the promotion of its own diversity – now have given rise to a new series of problems.

The country had been a loose confederation of sovereign cantons until 1798, when Napoleon's invasion transformed it into a "unitary and indivisible" republic in the image of France. After five years of rebellion and turmoil, the Emperor was forced to reinstate Switzerland's decentralized structure. Following the Congress of Vienna, the cantons, or constituent units, recovered full sovereignty. However, by the time of the Industrial Revolution this multitude of microstates in a loose confederation was so unworkable that it led to a brief civil war between the secessionist conservative Catholic (the Sonderbund) and the liberal Protestant cantons.

The country drew on its own vast experience in making the choice to adopt a federal system in its Constitution – the only system that could successfully unite 25 cantons (26 today) with extremely diverse characteristics. Indeed, this country, whose territory is 0.5 percent that of the United States, is home to four national languages, three main regions, and two major religions, without mentioning the many social differences between the cantons. The adoption of a federal system continued the tradition of a decentralized system that had existed since the first union of cantons in 1291. As a result, the former name of the country, the "Swiss Confederation," was retained, even though Switzerland is now a federation, rather than a confederation. The Constitution has served a delicate integrating function. By its commitment to diversity, it created a Willensnation – a country created from the will of its citizens to live together – in a territory seemingly unsuited to the creation of national sentiment.

> By its commitment to diversity, it created a *Willensnation* ... in a territory seemingly unsuited to the creation of national sentiment.

Like its American equivalent, the Swiss Constitution put an end to an unsatisfactory confederal system. Also like the American Constitution, it set up a bicameral parliament one of whose houses, the Council of States, represents the member cantons and is composed of two representatives from each. Finally, like the American Constitution, it has stood the test of time. Although it has undergone two total revisions, one in 1874 and more recently in 1999, along with more than 120 amendments endorsed by majorities in the federation and in a majority of the cantons, the institutions the Constitution originally established and the procedures it set up have remained essentially the same.

However, the Swiss Constitution deviates in several ways from the American Constitution, as it has had to accommodate the political, economic, social, and cultural diversity among and within the cantons. To do this, the Swiss Constitution provides for a unique collective executive called the Federal Council, composed of seven members from different cantons elected by both houses of parliament for a fixed term of four years. The council allows for the representation of the country's varied makeup. The President of Switzerland is simply one of the members of the Executive Council elected by the parliament with the position rotating annually.

The Swiss system has stabilized the country since 1848 without closing it off to innovations. It has subtly distributed power, sharing it among all the political actors in a country long accustomed to a system of cantons, municipalities, and direct democracy. Direct democracy entails the participation of the citizenry in governmental decisions, most often through the use of popular consultations and referenda and, at times, through direct voting on legislation. Although some federal powers have been enlarged, they have been limited through federalism and direct democracy, making Switzerland one of the most democratic countries in the world.

However, the price of these accomplishments is a constant search for consensus among all parties, resulting in a slow and difficult decision-making process in which compromise is considered an asset and not a weakness. Thus, although the Constitution saw Switzerland through the international wars and social upheaval of the twentieth century, the beginning of the twenty-first century has shaken what were traditionally thought to be certainties. It would appear that political leaders have focused on managing internal institutional equilibrium while neglecting economic and international challenges related to globalization and the migration of foreigners and asylum seekers.

The addition of ten new countries to the European Union on 1 May 2004 made Switzerland more than ever an island, or a hole, in the heart of the continent. Consequently, in May 2004, Swiss authorities and the European Union (EU) signed a second series of bilateral agreements. The length and complexity of the process demonstrated not only how delicate bilateral negotiations are, but also how dependent Switzerland is on the EU.

These matters are not the only ones troubling the country's famed stability. The October 2003 federal election signalled both a shift to the right and a polarization of the country's political climate. The election brought about the first change since 1959 in the party composition of the Federal Council, whose solidity had until then been so steadfast that the basis for representing parties was called the "magic formula." The resulting changing balance of parties in the government now raises questions about the Federal Council's relationship to parliament, and whether the council should be directly elected rather than chosen by parliament.

A further issue is the decision by German-speaking cantons to promote the teaching of English above that of French in compulsory education which could undermine national cohesion.

Finding solutions to these major political challenges will occupy constitutionalists, politicians, and citizens in the coming years. Denis de Rougemont, one of the leading European scholars of federalism in the twentieth century, praised the Swiss model for having created a "contented people" and having forged national unity by promoting its diversity. But will the complex decision-making processes for achieving consensus among Switzerland's diverse groups provide a solution or themselves prove to be the major problem?

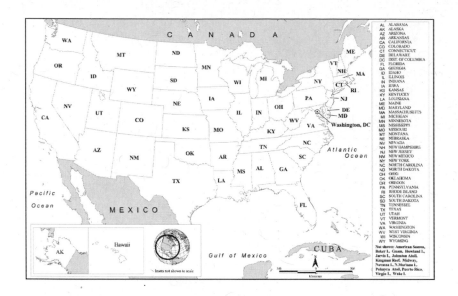

United States of America:
Enduring Constitution, New Challenges

G. ALAN TARR

In its successful history, the United States Constitution has served as both inspiration and model for emerging federal democracies around the world. It has proven itself capable of responding to past challenges – including a divisive civil war. Now, more than two-hundred years after its drafting, the U.S. Constitution is facing another crop of challenges.

One of the most significant questions is how the constitutional system can accommodate globalization, as illustrated by the adoption of the North America Free Trade Agreement (NAFTA) and by aggressive state involvement in trade policy. A continuing source of dispute is how the constitutional system should deal with differences among the states on crucial moral issues such as same-sex marriage, the death penalty, and abortion. Are these matters of fundamental right, such that a single national standard must prevail, or are these matters in which diversity among the states is constitutionally warranted? Another concern is how to guarantee an appropriate role for the states in the constitutional system, as reflected in debates over recent Supreme Court rulings on sovereign immunity and the commerce power that sought to safeguard the "dignity of the states."

While these ongoing challenges will continue to test the capacity of the United States' Constitution to adapt to change, history demonstrates that it has been a remarkably enduring document.

Created in 1787 after the failure of the Articles of Confederation, the country's first constitution, the Constitution has survived for more than two centuries. Over this period, the United States has changed dramatically: from 13 states clustered along the Atlantic seacoast to 50 states that span the continent (and in the case of Hawaii extend beyond it); from a relatively homogeneous country of a few million inhabitants to a diverse country of more than 270,000,000 people; and from a militarily and economically weak country to a superpower. Yet these changes have taken place largely within the confines of the Constitution – in more than two centuries, it has been amended only 27 times. What accounts for its extraordinary durability?

The answer lies in part in the Constitution's origins. The movement for a new constitution emerged less than a decade after independence from Great Britain, in reaction to the deficiencies of the Articles of Confederation. The Articles failed both to promote economic prosperity, as the country suffered from internal trade barriers, and to protect rights from mob rule both within and outside state legislatures. In addition, it did not produce the strong government necessary for the United States to play a role on the world stage. The founders remedied these problems both by augmenting the powers of the federal government and by granting the federal government the power to act directly on citizens. This shift from a confederal government acting on component units to a federal government acting on individuals marked a major innovation in federal theory that would influence later federal systems.

This shift from a confederal government acting on component units to a federal government acting on individuals marked a major innovation in federal theory that would influence later federal systems.

The Constitution resolved many problems but failed to confront the issue of slavery, which divided North and South. Some founders believed that slavery was economically inefficient and expected – or at least hoped – that it would gradually disappear. Others feared that confrontation on the issue would split the union, which it nearly did.

The Civil War itself was, in part, a constitutional conflict. The South insisted that the states had the right to order their own internal affairs (including whether or not to have slavery), whereas the North insisted that the Constitution's compromises with slavery were temporary and that the document should be read in light of the principles of the Declaration of Independence, referring to its celebrated line: "We hold these truths to be self-evident, that all men are created equal, that they are endowed by their Creator with certain unalienable Rights, that among these are Life, Liberty and the pursuit of Happiness." The South also viewed the union as a compact among states, with each state having the right to withdraw from the compact if it so desired, whereas the North viewed it as an indissoluble union of the people, even if organized in states. While the union did hold together, and the country's unity has never been seriously threatened since the Civil War, the Constitution underwent major transformations in its wake. The amendments adopted after the Civil War have had a "nationalizing" effect, albeit not one that has precluded federal diversity.

The success of the U.S. Constitution owes itself, in part, to allowing for common values on one hand, and flexibility for interpretation and state-level input on the other. A distinctive aspect of the U.S. federal Constitution is a lack of detail in many (though not all) of its provisions. This generality permits a certain "play in the joints," affording future generations a role in constitutional design. When one compares the U.S. federal Constitution to its counterpart in other federal democracies, one is also struck by the fact that the U.S. Constitution leaves a great deal of choice about governance to the states. Each order of government is primarily responsible for designing its own institutions and raising its own revenues, and the Constitution does not prescribe a system of transfer payments. Local government, education, health care, and housing – all topics dealt with in most countries' federal constitutions – receive no express mention in the U.S. federal Constitution, though state constitutions deal with them in considerable detail. However, this lack of detail does not preclude the federal government from acting effectively.

Although the Constitution grants the federal government only limited powers, those powers enable it to perform its constitutionally prescribed functions, and it has all powers "necessary and proper" for carrying its granted powers into effect. Moreover, the federal government retains authority to legislate for individuals, and so it does not have to rely on state governments to carry out its policies. Furthermore, the federal government has expanded its powers considerably. Broad interpretation of federal powers, such as the power to regulate commerce, combined with the use of the spending power to pursue aims that could not be pursued directly under the powers granted to the federal government, have contributed to this expansion. This federal expansion does not necessarily mean a diminution of state responsibility, rather, it reflects the fact that the scope of responsibilities has increased on all levels of government.

Comparative Reflections

G. ALAN TARR

Every country's constitution is somewhat distinctive, a reflection of the country's history, culture, and character of its populace. Nonetheless, as the preceding articles have shown, there are significant commonalities among constitutions as well. In many instances, the resemblances that one finds among constitutions are the product of design, not of chance. Because constitution-making represents the most fundamental exercise of political choice, constitution-makers are well advised to seek the broadest possible perspective on the task in which they are engaged. Thus, countries devising new constitutional regimes characteristically look to the experience of other countries, learning from their successes and their failures, and borrowing from them, even while adapting what they have learned to the circumstances within their own borders. One can scarcely overstate the importance of this process of learning, borrowing, and adapting for informed deliberation on constitutional matters. By presenting snapshots of constitutional arrangements and developments in 12 federal democracies, these articles furnish public officials and citizens with a useful guide to constitutional design and constitutional practice in federal democracies.

In part, the common features found in constitutions reflect the fact that a constitution plays a distinct function in a country's political life. A constitution embodies a country's fundamental choices about government, and in some countries – Brazil, South Africa, and the United States, for example – its creation is a source of pride and a symbol of national unity for citizens. The constitution also designates offices and specifies how those offices are to be filled. It allocates power among the various offices and indicates the aims for which political power is to be exercised. In most countries it also establishes limits on the exercise of government power, most obviously by elaborating rights that are to be secured against violation by government.

When a country adopts a federal system, the tasks of the federal constitution are multiplied. In addition to the functions mentioned above, the constitution in a federal system determines what the component units of the federal system are. It may establish two orders of government, as is found in Germany and the United States, with local governments created by and controlled by the constituent governments. Or it may institute a three-order federal system, as in Nigeria, Russia, and South Africa, giving constitutional status to local governments and guaranteeing them certain powers. Or it may devise a more complex variation, as in Belgium's double federation of language communities and territorial units.

The federal constitution also decides what role the component units will play in the structure and operation of the federal government. In most federal systems, the component units participate in the process of constitutional amendment, illustrated by both Australia's and Switzerland's requirements that amendments be approved in a referendum by a majority of voters nationally and a majority in a majority of the states. Many federal systems also ensure a further role for the component units by creating a bicameral federal legislature, with the upper (federal) chamber representing – and often elected by – the component units of the federation. Indeed, reformers seeking to enhance federalism in both Canada and Mexico have focused on creating a stronger role for the federal chamber. Switzerland has gone the farthest in securing participation of the component units in the federal government, establishing a multi-member executive composed of representatives from seven different cantons.

The federal constitution also determines the range of discretion available to the component units of the federal system in creating their own polities. Federal systems differ in the extent to which they allow component units to determine their form of government, the purposes for which they will exercise political power, and the rights that they will protect. In India and Nigeria, for example, the component units do not have free-standing subnational constitutions. Decisions about the structure and operation of the governments of the component units are enshrined in the federal constitution, which can be said to "include" the subnational constitutions, or contained in federal legislation. By contrast, in Australia and the United States (among others), the component units devise and revise their own constitutions. States in Brazil and Mexico also have some room to devise and revise their constitutions, but many details of state government are prescribed by the federal constitution. Russia and South Africa have pioneered special arrangements. In Russia, some component units (republics) are authorized to create their own constitutions, while others (e.g., regions) can only devise charters.

In South Africa, provinces can adopt provincial constitutions, but they are not obliged to do so, and in fact only one province (Western Cape) has availed itself of the option.

More generally, the federal constitution allocates power between the federal government and the constituent governments. The federal systems described in this volume differ dramatically in their degree of centralization. Federal systems engaged in the task of social and economic transformation – such as India and South Africa – have tended to choose a highly centralized federalism. The recent centralizing reforms by President Vladimir Putin in Russia show the attractiveness of this model for countries undertaking fundamental change. In contrast, federal systems seeking to accommodate diversity within their populations – such as Belgium and Switzerland – have usually opted for a more decentralized federalism. Obviously, there is no optimum degree of centralization or decentralization; the circumstances within the particular society should be decisive. Nevertheless, it is interesting that the studies of Canada, Germany, and Nigeria in this volume all point to problems associated with excessive centralization and stress the need for devolution of power.

In allocating powers, a constitution determines what powers are the exclusive prerogative of each government and what powers are shared or concurrent. The federal constitution also defines how conflicts among the governments regarding the distribution of powers are to be resolved. Both concurrency and separate spheres can lead to problems. When powers are divided between the federal government and the component units, the federal constitution typically provides a mechanism for policing the division of authority, usually a constitutional court or a supreme court. The rulings of the judicial umpire can then dramatically alter the federal balance, encouraging a greater centralization of power (as occurred in Brazil and, until recently, in the United States) or a greater decentralization (as in Canada). Moreover, a constitution that emphasizes separate spheres for the federal and component governments may discourage the sorts of intergovernmental coordination necessary for addressing problems, as was pointed out in the study of Brazil's constitution. Yet when powers are shared (concurrent), this can lead to federal dominance over policymaking. Most federal systems recognize the supremacy of federal law over that of the component units, giving a hierarchical cast to cooperative arrangements. Although the creation of concurrent powers usually was meant to allow the federal government to craft framework legislation, while ensuring component units considerable discretion within the framework, in practice – as the experiences of Russia and South Africa suggest – detailed federal legislation may leave little room for initiatives by the constituent governments. The tendency toward federal dominance may be particularly strong in systems in which the federal government dominates the collection and distribution of tax revenues, as in Germany and India.

The drafters of a constitution may establish a division of authority between the federal government and the component units, but that division is likely to evolve over time in response to developments both within the country and beyond its borders. Several broad factors have contributed – and will continue to contribute – to changes in federal constitutions and the federal systems they govern, producing either new constitutions or changes within existing arrangements. Some of the most important developments have been economic, as federal constitutions have sought to accommodate and manage the shift from localized to national economies and, more recently, the shift to globalization. Political changes have also had a significant impact. The development of the European Union has dramatically affected European federations, and democratization has provided an impetus for new or revived federations in Africa, in the former Soviet bloc, and in Latin America. Finally, the resurgence of ethnic, linguistic, and religious loyalties has created challenges for virtually all federal systems, as they seek to combine unity and diversity.

Some mature federal democracies – for example, Australia and India – have created durable constitutions that have not required fundamental reform. The United States might have fit into that category too, had its history not been punctuated by a civil war and by constitutional changes flowing from that conflict. Another long-standing federal democracy, Switzerland, adopted a new constitution in 1999, but it did so while retaining its constitutional foundations.

Other mature federal democracies have had to confront new challenges to their constitutional orders. In the wake of reunification, Germany has had to deal with the economic backwardness of the "new *Länder*," and this has led to calls to re-examine the federal structure and particularly the system of fiscal equalization. In Canada, the rise of separatist sentiments in Quebec led in the 1980s and 1990s to "mega-constitutional" politics in which Canadians debated a series of proposals to radically restructure their constitution. Although none of those proposals eventually won approval, the adoption of the Charter of Rights and Freedoms in 1982 inaugurated a fundamental constitutional shift in Canada.

Other federal democracies are involved in the difficult task of creating a durable constitutional order after a period of dictatorship. In some instances – for example, Russia in 1993 and South Africa in 1996 – the new constitutions represent the country's attempt to fashion a viable constitutional democracy. In other instances – for example, Brazil since 1988 and Nigeria since 1999 – the challenge is to restore constitutional democracy after previous constitutional arrangements failed or were overthrown, leading to military dictatorship. The success of these federal democracies will depend on their ability to solve the economic problems and ethnic conflicts that they inherited from those dictatorships.

Finally, some federal democracies, such as Belgium and Mexico, are in the midst of significant constitutional changes that are designed to strengthen the authority of the component units of those federations. In Belgium, however, the aim is to ensure that devolutions of power to the component units do not trigger ethno-linguistic cleavages that will lead to the dissolution of the country. In Mexico, the aim is to revitalize federalism after a long period of dominance by a federal government controlled by a single political party. Whatever the outcome of these efforts, there is no doubt that they can serve as guides – or cautionary lessons – to citizens, eager to learn how their counterparts in other countries have addressed common problems and concerns.

Timeline of Constitutional Events

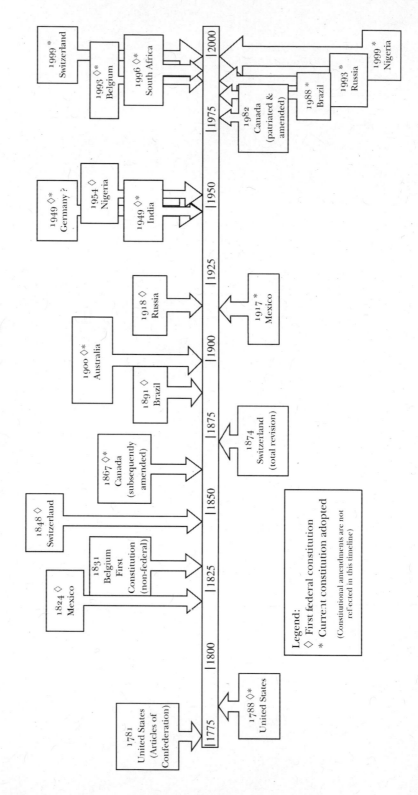

Legend:
◇ First federal constitution
* Current constitution adopted
(Constitutional amendments are not reflected in this timeline)

1781 United States (Articles of Confederation)

1788 ◇* United States

1824 ◇ Mexico

1831 Belgium First Constitution (non-federal)

1848 ◇ Switzerland

1867 ◇* Canada (subsequently amended)

1874 Switzerland (total revision)

1891 ◇ Brazil

1900 ◇* Australia

1917 * Mexico

1918 ◇ Russia

1949 ◇* Germany ?

1954 ◇ Nigeria

1949 ◇* India

1982 Canada (patriated & amended)

1988 * Brazil

1993 Russia

1999 * Nigeria

1999 * Switzerland

1993 ◇* Belgium

1996 ◇* South Africa

1775 1800 1825 1850 1875 1900 1925 1950 1975 2000

Glossary

ABORIGINALS   1. original inhabitants of a country or territory; replaces the expression "Indians" in Canada (though not in USA). Also Aboriginal peoples. 2. Original inhabitants of Australia; replaces Aborigines.

ADMINISTRATIVE REGION   reference to a territory under colonial administration.

APARTHEID   legal framework of racial segregation and discrimination against non-Europeans in South Africa (1948 to early 1990s).

ARTICLES OF CONFEDERATION (AND PERPETUAL UNION)   first constitution of the United States of America, 1781–88.

ASYMMETRICAL FEDERALISM   denotes unequal or non-identical distribution of powers and responsibilities between the constituent units of a federal system.

BASIC LAW   'constitution'; literal translation of *grundgesetz*, the constitution of the Federal Republic of Germany.

BICAMERAL   denotes legislature composed of two chambers.

BILL OF RIGHTS   a constitutional or quasi-constitutional document of fundamental rights; from the so-called Bill of Rights in the United States of America, the first ten amendments to the US Constitution. Also: charter of rights.

BUNDESRAT   [German] Federal Council; the upper house or second chamber of the bicameral national legislature of Germany.

BUNDESREPUBLIK DEUTSCHLAND   [German] Federal Republic of Germany; official name of West Germany and, subsequently, unified Germany.

BUNDESTAG   [German] Federal Assembly; the popularly-elected lower house or first chamber of the bicameral national legislature of Germany.

CANTON   name for the 26 constituent units in the Swiss federation.

CASTES   hereditary social and religious hierarchical status groups in India.

CENTRALISM   concentration of powers and responsibilities at the national level of government.

CHAMBER OF DEPUTIES   lower house or first chamber in the bicameral national legislatures of Belgium, Brazil, and Mexico.

CHAMBER OF SENATORS   upper house or second chamber in the bicameral national legislature of Mexico.

CHARLOTTETOWN ACCORD   1992 intergovernmental agreement on constitutional reform in Canada; abandoned as a result of failure to win majority support in a national referendum.

CHARTER OF RIGHTS   see bill of rights.

CHARTER OF RIGHTS AND FREEDOMS   the Canadian bill of rights entrenched in the *Constitution Act 1982.*

CHECHEN CASE   1995 decision by the Russian Constitutional Court allowing the use of military force to intervene in separatist conflicts (e.g., in the Chechen republic).

CHECHEN REPUBLIC   a constituent unit of the Russian federation with a violent separatist movement and ongoing military intervention.

CIVIL LAW   body of private law developed from Roman law and based on statute or code; as distinguished from common law based on precedent; see common law.

COMMERCE POWER/CLAUSE   one of Congress's enumerated powers under Article I, section 8 of the US Constitution, the power "To regulate Commerce with foreign Nations, and among the several State ..." Primary constitutional basis for the centralization of American federalism.

COMMON LAW   British tradition of a legal system based on accumulated judicial decisions known as precedent and diffused through the English-speaking world. Contrast with statute or civil code law; see civil law.

COMMONWEALTH   1. British Commonwealth of nations, a loose association of sovereign states originally under British control. 2. Australia's national government as distinct from the governments of the Australian states.

COMMONWEALTH OF AUSTRALIA   official name of Australia.

COMMUNES À FACILITÉS   [French] linguistic communities that are minority populations within Belgian regions and have protected language rights.

COMMUNITIES   in Belgium the term for the language-based divisions of the system that operate in parallel with the territorially-based regions.

COMPACT   a contractual agreement between two or more political units in which the contracting parties retain primacy and any participating member is characteristically seen as retaining the right to withdraw.

COMPETITIVE FEDERALISM   the idea that the constituent governments of a federation should compete with each other, and with the national government, in order to enhance overall socioeconomic efficiency and effectiveness in the delivery of public services.

CONCURRENT POWERS   an approach to dividing powers whereby orders of government are implicitly or explicitly expected to share jurisdiction over specific policy areas. Can be effected either by creating a list of shared powers, or by granting authority over various functions to one order of government without providing for those powers to be exclusive.

CONFEDERAL SYSTEM OF GOVERNMENT   a confederacy or confederation is a limited or decentralized form of union where the constituent units retain the bulk of their sovereignty and enjoy the primary relationship to the people while a national government of certain limited functions operates largely on the basis of delegated powers.

CONGRESS   the bicameral national legislature of the presidential system of government in the United States of America. Prior to that, the unicameral and sole governing body of the United States under the Articles of Confederation.

CONGRESS OF THE UNION   the bicameral national legislature of the presidential system of government in Mexico; also Federal Congress.

CONSTITUENT UNIT   a constitutionally recognized member unit of a federation.

CONSTITUTION ACT, 1867   the first and, as amended, continuing current constitution of Canada; formerly entitled British North America Act, 1867.

CONSTITUTION ACT, 1982   an amendment to the Constitution Act 1867 adding a Charter of Rights and Freedoms and a domestic procedure for constitutional amendment in Canada (rather than by the United Kingdom Parliament).

CONSTITUTIONAL COURT   a judicial body exercising final jurisdiction specifically over constitutional questions including the relationship between orders of government in a federation, as distinct from a "supreme court" or one that acts as the apex of the legal system in general. First established in Austria; examples now include Belgium's Court of Arbitration (*Cour d'arbitrage*), Germany's Federal Constitutional Court (*Bundesverfassungsgericht*), and the constitutional courts of South Africa and the Russian Federation.

CONSTITUTIONAL HIERARCHY   rule that the national constitution is superior to those of the constituent units; also: supremacy clause.

CONSTITUTIONAL MONARCHY   historically a system where royal authority was not absolute but limited by a constitutional framework; now refers to the vestigial existence of monarchical heads of state in parliamentary democracies (e.g., Australia, Canada).

COOPERATIVE FEDERALISM   practice and principle of modern federalism whereby the orders of government work together to coordinate policy design and delivery in areas of overlapping responsibility. Prescribed in some federations (e.g., Germany's "joint tasks") but more typically an adaptive response of governments to the realities of modern federal governance. Does not necessarily entail an equality of power and resources between the participating orders of government and indeed may represent an exercise in coercive federalism whereby the superior resources or powers of the federal government impose national policies.

COUNCIL OF THE FEDERATION   1. upper house or second chamber in the bicameral national legislature of the Russian Federation; also Federation Council. 2. Recently adopted as title for the meeting of provincial heads of government in Canada.

COUNCIL OF STATES   1. *Ständerat*; upper house or second chamber in the bicameral national legislature of Switzerland. 2. one of several intergovernmental bodies for conflict resolution under the Nigerian Constitution.

CROWN   formal expression of sovereign authority in countries such as Canada and Australia with a vestigial monarchy.

DEMOCRATIC CENTRALISM   Marxist-Leninist doctrine according to which democracy is compatible with one-party rule.

DEVOLUTION OF POWERS   transfer of powers and responsibilities from a central government to subordinate entities; not necessarily based on constitutional change.

DISTRIBUTION OF AUTHORITY   constitutional allocation of legislative and executive powers among different orders of government (also: division of authority; division of powers).

DIRECT DEMOCRACY   involvement of the citizenry in law-making as an alternative or supplement to government by elected representatives; notably in Switzerland through ratification of legislation and constitutional amendments by referendums or initiation of legislation by popular action; also "semi-direct" as indication that it complements, not supercedes, representative democracy.

DISTINCT SOCIETY   a political term used to describe the province of Quebec in Canada as unique in terms culture and language; constitutional adoption of the term failed.

DOUBLE FEDERATION   a federation consisting of two different types of constituent units (notably: language communities and territorial regions in Belgium).

DUAL FEDERALISM   the idea of strict legislative separation of powers in a federation; each order of government legislates and administers autonomously in its own sphere. Also: watertight compartments.

DUMA   [Russian] see State Duma.

ENGLISH CANADA   refers collectively to the English-speaking community of Canada; see French Canada.

EQUAL REPRESENTATION   the same number of representatives from regions or constituent units regardless of population; usually in second chambers.

ETHNO-FEDERALISM   type of federalism recognizing ethnic communities as constituent entities.

EXECUTIVE FEDERALISM   in parliamentary federations (e.g., Canada, Australia, India) the prevalence of intergovernmental negotiation conducted between and within orders of government by the political executive, largely to the exclusion of the legislative branch.

FEDERAL ASSEMBLY   1. bicameral national legislature of Switzerland (*Bundesversammlung*). 2. bicameral national legislature of Russia (*Federalnoye Sobraniye*). 3. lower house of the bicameral national legislature of Germany (*Bundestag*).

FEDERAL CHANCELLOR   *Bundeskanzler*; the head of government in the parliamentary system of the Federal Republic of Germany.

FEDERAL CITY   *federalny gorod*; a city with the constitutional status of a province in the Russian federation (e.g., Moscow, St. Petersburg).

FEDERAL CONSTITUTIONAL COURT   *Bundesverfassungsgericht*; the final judicial body on matters of constitutional law in Germany. See constitutional court.

FEDERAL CONSTITUTIONAL SUPREMACY   see constitutional hierarchy.

FEDERAL COUNCIL   1. upper house or second chamber in the bicameral national legislatures of both Germany and Austria (*Bundesrat*). 2. Executive governing council and collective head of state in Switzerland *(Bundesrat/Conseil fédéral/Consiglio federale)*. 3. upper house or second chamber of the bicameral national legislature of the Russian Federation (*Sovet Federatsii*).

FEDERAL DISTRICT   a term used for a capital region with special status in a federation (e.g., District of Columbia in the United States of America; Federal District of Brasilia in Brazil).

FEDERAL PARLIAMENT   name of the bicameral national legislatures of Australia, Belgium, Brazil, Canada, Germany, India, and South Africa.

FEDERAL SENATE   upper house or chamber in the bicameral legislature of Brazil.

FEDERAL SUPREME COURT   the highest court of Switzerland.

FEDERATED ENTITY   a political unit united in a federation (see also constituent unit).

FEDERATION   1. a form of governement in which powers are constitutionally divided among two or more orders of government; typically a federal state. 2. the process of forming such a government.

FIRST MINISTERS   refers to the Prime Minister of Canada and the 13 premiers (heads of government) of the 13 provinces and territories of Canada.

FIRST NATIONS   those of Canada's indigenous people who had "treaty Indian" status.

FOUNDING NATIONS   originally used to refer to French and English as 'first' settlers in Canada, but now regarded as failing to recognize Aboriginals as prior occupants of the land.

FRANCOPHONE   1. person whose native language is French. 2. person in a plurilingual society whose native language is French (e.g., in Canada).

FRENCH CANADA refers to population of Canada for whom French is the first language; located mainly in Quebec, parts of New Brunswick, parts of Ontario, and smaller settlements in other provinces.

GERMAN DEMOCRATIC REPUBLIC (GDR)   official name of East Germany (1949–1989).

GOROD   [Russian] see federal city.

GOSUDARSTVENNAYA DUMA   [Russian] see State Duma.

GOVERNOR-GENERAL   the vice-regal head of state in Australia and Canada; officially the appointed representative of the Queen.

GOVERNOR   commonly the title of the elected head of a subnational constituent unit of a federation, such as in the case of the United States (state governor) or Russia (regional governor).

GRUNDGESETZ   [German] Basic Law; the constitution of the Federal Republic of Germany.

HIGH COURT OF AUSTRALIA   the supreme court for constitutional and other law in the Commonwealth of Australia.

HOUSE OF COMMONS   lower house of the bicameral national legislature of Canada.

HOUSE OF REPRESENTATIVES   name of the lower house or first chamber in the bicameral national legislatures of Australia, Nigeria, and the United States; sometimes used as the translation for the names of the lower houses of the Belgian, German, and Swiss legislatures.

INDIGENE   termed coined for the original inhabitants of a specific locale in Nigeria as distinct from newcomers from other regions within the country.

INDIGENESHIP RIGHTS   constitutional rights for indigene populations in Nigeria.

INDIGENOUS PEOPLES   generic term for the original inhabitants of a country or region; see Aboriginals.

INTERGOVERNMENTAL RELATIONS   relations between the governments of constituent units or between various orders of governments for the purpose of policy coordination and/or agreement on shared programs etc.

JUDICIAL REVIEW   power of the courts to decide upon the constitutionality of legislative or executive acts.

JUDICIAL INTERPRETATION   role of the courts in establishing precise meanings of constitutional provisions or legislative acts.

LAND   [German] name for the 16 constituent units of the German federation; *Länder* plural.

LANGUAGE COMMUNITY   refers to the three self-governing cultural communities, as distinct from the territorial regions, in the Belgian federation.

LEVELS OF GOVERNMENT   see orders of government.

LOK SABHA   [Hindi] People's Assembly; lower house or first chamber of the bicameral national legislature of India.

MAGIC FORMULA   1959 power-sharing agreement on the distribution of seats in the Swiss Federal Council among the 4 major parties; modified in 2003.

MEECH LAKE ACCORD   1987 intergovernmental agreement on constitutional change in Canada; ratification failed; see distinct society.

MEXICAN REVOLUTION   pivotal popular uprising in Mexican history, eventually leading to the Constitution of 1917.

MULTICULTURALISM   a concept or policy committed to the toleration and protection of cultural diversity within a country (e.g., Australia, Canada).

NATIONAL ASSEMBLY   lower house or first chamber in the bicameral national legislatures of Nigeria and South Africa.

NATIONAL AUTONOMOUS DISTRICT   name of 10 constituent units in the Russian federation.

NATIONAL AUTONOMOUS PROVINCE   name of one constituent unit in the Russian federation.

NATIONAL CONGRESS   the bicameral national legislature in the presidential system of government in Brazil.

NATIONAL COUNCIL   *Nationalrat/Conseil national/Consiglio nazionale*; lower house or first chamber in the bicameral national legislature of Switzerland.

NATIONAL COUNCIL OF PROVINCES   upper house or second chamber in the bicameral national legislature of South Africa.

NATIONAL JUDICIAL COUNCIL   a federal body in Nigeria having the power over the appointment, promotion, discipline, and funding of the country's judiciary.

NATIONAL REPUBLICS   name for 21 of the 89 constituent units in the Russian federation. See: subjects of the federation.

NECESSARY AND PROPER   the final clause of Article I, section 8 of the US Constitution listing the powers of Congress; broadens scope of enumerated powers by allowing Congress "To make all Laws which shall be necessary and proper for carrying into Execution the foregoing Powers" and has been integral to the centralization of the US federal system.

NORTH AMERICAN FREE TRADE AGREEMENT (NAFTA)   a set of bilateral treaties establishing the rules for a free trade relationship between Canada, the United States, and Mexico.

ORDERS OF GOVERNMENT   the various levels of government in a federation; typically one overarching central government, several broad regional governments that are the constituent units, and a multitude of local governments, notably municipalities; however, may be more complex (e.g., Russia).

PANCHAYATS   municipal bodies or local governments in rural areas in India.

PARLIAMENT   the legislature in any country where the political executive is formed in and answerable to the legislature (e.g., Australia, Canada, Germany, India, and South Africa). May be used for national legislature exclusively or for legislatures of constituent units as well (Australia).

PATRIATION   addition of a domestic amending formula into the Canadian Constitution by the Constitution Act, 1982; thereby ending dependence on external United Kingdom legislation for Canadian constitutional changes.

PEOPLE'S ASSEMBLY   *lok sabha*; lower house or first chamber in the bicameral national legislature of India.

PLURALITY VOTE   method of determining a winner in an election without requiring a majority of votes, merely more votes than any other single candidate; Also: "first past-the-post".

PRESIDENT   the head of state in non-monarchical parliamentary systems (e.g., in Germany, India) and mixed systems (South Africa, Russia, Switzerland); or combined head of state and head of government in presidential systems (e.g., Brazil, Mexico, Nigeria, United States of America).

PRINCIPLE OF TERRITORIALITY   primary recognition given to geographically defined units rather than other bases of identity.

PRIME MINISTER   head of government in parliamentary systems (e.g., Australia, Belgium, Canada, India).

PROPORTIONAL REPRESENTATION   method of assigning seats in a legislature in proportion to the share of votes received by the contesting parties by means of nation-wide or regional multi-member electoral districts. Also: PR.

PROVINCE   name for constituent units, as an alternative to states, in various federations (Canada, 10 provinces; South Africa, 9 provinces; Russia, 49 provinces); in some federations used for divisions below the level of the constituent units (e.g., Spain).

PROVINCIAL EQUALITY   denotes equal or symmetrical distribution of powers and responsibilities among all provinces in a federation.

RAJYA SABHA   [Hindi] Assembly of States; upper house or second chamber of the bicameral Indian national legislature.

REGION   term for the three territorial units in Belgium (Wallonia, Flanders, Brussels).

REPUBLIC   1. principal constituent unit in the Russian federation. 2. system of government where political power is exercised by those directly or indirectly elected by the people, including the head of state.

RESPONSIBLE GOVERNMENT   the British or 'Westminster' term for an executive government that is accountable to the people via the people's elected representatives in parliament (i.e., a parliamentary democracy).

RESIDUAL POWERS   those unidentified powers that are left by a federal constitution either implicitly or explicitly to a particular order of government in contrast to explicitly assigned enumerated powers.

RUSSIAN SOCIALIST FEDERATED SOVIET REPUBLIC (RSFSR)   official name of Russia from 1918 until 1924 before joining the Union of Soviet Socialist Republics (USSR).

SECESSION   withdrawal of a constituent unit from a federation.

SECOND CHAMBER   the chamber in a bicameral legislature that provides for representation on other than a strict democratic population basis; in federations the chamber that provides for representation of the constituent units in some way.

SELF-GOVERNMENT   denotes a claim or right of autonomy or self-rule; enshrined for Aboriginal peoples in the Canadian *Constitution Act 1982*.

SENATE   name of the upper house or second chamber in the bicameral national legislatures of Australia, Belgium, Brazil, Canada, Nigeria, Mexico, and United States of America.

SHARIAH LAW   code of Islamic law in force in some northern states of Nigeria.

SOVEREIGN IMMUNITY   principle of constitutionalism in the United States of America that the states ought to enjoy an immunity from national interference in their own governments as a correlate of their semi-sovereign status.

SPENDING POWER   the ability of the central government in a federation to exercise influence or control over matters falling within the jurisdiction of the lower order governments by means of its superior financial resources; operates either through the power to fund national programs or through the power to make transfers conditional upon adherence to national norms.

STÄNDERAT   [German] Council of States; the upper house or second chamber of the bicameral national legislature of Switzerland.

STATES   name for the constituent units in the federations of Australia (6 states), Brazil (26 states), India (28 states), Mexico (31 states), Nigeria (36 states), United States of America (50 states).

STATE DUMA   *Gosudarstvennaya Duma*, 'National Council'; lower house or first chamber in the bicameral national legislature of Russia.

SUB-CASTE   a subordinate division of a caste; see castes.

SUBJECTS OF THE FEDERATION   generic reference to the 89 varying constituent units of the Russian federation, comprising republics, territories, regions, autonomous areas, autonomous regions, and federal cities.

SUBSIDIARITY   principle according to which every task should be performed at the lowest possible level of governance where the task can be adequately performed.

SUPREMACY CLAUSE   generically, a constitutional clause stipulating the superiority of national law over the laws of the constituent units in a federation; specifically, Article VI, clause 2 of the US Constitution.

SUPREME COURT   the highest court for constitutional and other law in Canada, India, Mexico, Nigeria, and the United States.

SUPREME FEDERAL TRIBUNAL   the highest court in Brazil.

SUPREME LAW OF THE UNION   the federal Constitution of Mexico, the laws of the Congress of the Union that derive from it, and international treaties under Article 133 of the Mexican Constitution.

SWISS CONFEDERATION   official name of Switzerland – notwithstanding the reality that since 1848 it has been a true federation rather than a confederation.

SYMMETRICAL FEDERALISM   denotes equal or identical distribution of powers and responsibilities between and across any order of government in a federal system.

TERRITORIAL FEDERALISM   the conventional division of federal systems into geographically defined sub-units rather than linguistic, cultural, ethnic, occupational, or other bases of identity.

TERRITORIES   name for units in a federation that do not have the constitutional status of constituent units (by contrast with provinces, states, etc.); may or may not be self-governing (2 self-governing territories in Australia, 3 in Canada, 1 in Nigeria, 6 in Russia). See Union Territories.

THIRD ORDER OF GOVERNMENT   reference to self-governing units below central government and constituent units of a federation; of inferior or non-existent constitutional status (typically municipalities, but also Aboriginal peoples).

UNION   1. informal reference to a federation as a whole, or to the national order of governance. 2. official term for the Indian federation.

UNION TERRITORIES   name for six territorial units of India.

UNITARY STATE   a state with a single centre of sovereign political authority as opposed to a federal state; can be centralized or decentralized but decentralized regional or local governments do not have constitutionally protected status.

UNIVERSAL SOCIAL SERVICES   public social services equally available to all citizens.

WILLENSNATION   [German] term referring to the formation of the Swiss federation via a deliberate act of popular will rather than a natural expression of national sentiment or identity.

Contributors

IGNATIUS AKAAYAR AYUA, solicitor general, Federal Republic of Nigeria

RAOUL BLINDENBACHER, vice president, Forum of Federations, Canada/Switzerland

BARBARA BROOK, program manager, Global Dialogue program, Forum of Federations, Canada

KRIS DESCHOUWER, professor of politics, Vrije Universiteit Brussel, Belgium

JUAN MARCOS GUTIÉRREZ GONZÁLEZ, consul general of Mexico, Denver, Colorado, USA/Mexico

RAINER KNOPFF, professor of political science and associate vice president, Research and International, University of Calgary, Canada

JUTTA KRAMER, lawyer and senior research assistant, Institute for Federal Studies, University of Hanover, Germany

KATY LE ROY, assistant director, Centre for Comparative Constitutional Studies, University of Melbourne, Australia

AKHTAR MAJEED, professor of political science and director of the Centre for Federal Studies, Hamdard University, New Delhi, India

ABIGAIL OSTIEN, communications coordinator, Global Dialogue program, Forum of Federations, Canada

MARAT SALIKOV, director to the dean, Institute of Justice of Urals State Law Academy and professor, Urals State Law Academy, Yekaterinburg, Russia

CHERYL SAUNDERS, professor of law, University of Melbourne, Australia; president, International Association of Constitutional Law; and president, International Association of Centers for Federal Studies

ANTHONY SAYERS, associate professor of political science, University of Calgary, Canada

NICOLAS SCHMITT, research fellow, Institute on Federalism, University of Fribourg, Switzerland

CELINA SOUZA, professor and researcher of political science and public administration, Federal University of Bahia, Brazil

NICO STEYTLER, director of the Community Law Centre, University of the Western Cape, South Africa

G. ALAN TARR, director of the Center for State Constitutional Studies and chair of the Department of Political Science, Rutgers University-Camden, United States of America

Participants of the Global Dialogue on Federalism

We gratefully acknowledge the assistance of the following experts who participated in the theme of Constitutional Origins, Structure, and Change. While participants contributed their knowledge and experience, they are in no way responsible for the contents of this booklet.

José Roberto Afonso, Brazil
Basília Aguirre, Brazil
Peter Akper, Nigeria
Chris Alcantara, Canada
E. Alemika, Nigeria
Zinaida Alexandrova, Russia
Miguel Ángel Romo, Mexico
Marta Arretche, Brazil
Jean-François Aubert, Switzerland
Céline Auclair, Canada
I.A. Ayua, Nigeria
E.C.J. Azinge, Nigeria
Janet Azjenstat, Canada
Lynn Baker, United States
Gérald Beaudoin, Canada
Wouter Beke, Belgium
Svetlana Bendyurina, Russia
Gilberto Bercovici, Brazil
C.P. Bhambri, India
Vladimir Boublik, Russia
Dirk Brand, South Africa
Claudine Brohi, Switzerland
A.J. Brown, Australia
César Camacho Quiroz, Mexico

Jaime Cárdenas Gracia, Mexico
Siska Castelein, Belgium
Octavio Chavez, Mexico
Jan Clement, Belgium
Jamison Colburn, United States
Barry Cooper, Canada
Fernando Cosenza, Brazil
Juan José Crispín Borbolla, Mexico
David De Groot, Canada
Kris Deschouwer, Belgium
Hugues Dumont, Belgium
Alex Ekwueme, Nigeria
Vanessa Elias de Oliveira, Brazil
Rebeca Elizalde Hernández, Mexico
Fred Erdman, Belgium
Simon Evans, Australia
Patrick Fafard, Canada
James Faulkner, Australia
Carlos Figueiredo, Brazil
Thomas Fleiner, Switzerland
Rubén Jaime Flores Medina, Mexico
Stephen Frank, United States
Carlos Gadsden Carrazco, Mexico
Brian Galligan, Australia

Roger Gibbins, Canada
Tatiana Gladkova, Russia
Leslie Goldstein, United States
Manuel González Oropeza, Mexico
Karthy Govender, South Africa
Michael Grant, Mexico
Tonatiuh Guillén López, Mexico
Desiree Guobadia, Nigeria
Juan Marcos Gutiérrez González, Mexico
Geoffrey Hale, Canada
Ian Harris, Australia
N. Hembe, Nigeria
Simone Hermans, South Africa
Jan Martin Hoffmann, Germany
Meenakshi Hooja, India
Javier Hurtado González, Mexico
Gennady Ignatenko, Russia
R.B. Jain, India
César Jáuregui Robles, Mexico
Harold Jensen, Canada
Nirmal Jindal, India
B.B. Kanyip, Nigeria
Subhash C. Kashyap, India
Ellis Katz, United States
Cristiane Kersches, Brazil
Arshi Khan, India
Farah Khan, India
John Kincaid, United States
Paul King, Canada
Rainer Knopff, Canada
Alexander Kokotov, Russia
Royce Koop, Canada
Jutta Kramer, Germany
Christopher Kukucha, Canada
T. Ladan, Nigeria
Nicolas Lagasse, Belgium
Natalia Larionova, Russia
Harvey Lazar, Canada
Katy Le Roy, Australia
Dörte Liebetruth, Germany
Geoffrey Lindell, Australia
Marina Lomovtseva, Russia

Augustin Macheret, Switzerland
Akhtar Majeed, India
Christopher Manfredi, Canada
Preston Manning, Canada
Bernardo H. Martínez Aguirre, Mexico
George Mathew, India
David McCann, Australia
Peter McCormick, Canada
Nadezhda Mershina, Russia
Geraldine Mettler, South Africa
Hans Michelmann, Canada
Adrián Miranda, Mexico
Eamon Morann, Australia
F.L. Morton, Canada
Radinaledi Mosiane, South Africa
Christina Murray, South Africa
Marie Nagy, Belgium
A.S. Narang, India
Svetlana Nesmeyanova, Russia
Valeri Nevinski, Russia
A.G. Noorani, India
Charles-Ferdinand Nothomb, Belgium
Ofem Obno-Obla, Nigeria
Alessandro Octaviani, Brazil
Lawal Olayinka, Nigeria
Donald David Onje, Nigeria
Brian Opeskin, Australia
Waldeck Ornelas, Brazil
Sam Oyovbaire, Nigeria
Francisco José Paoli Bolio, Mexico
Victor Perevalov, Russia
Javier Pérez Torres, Mexico
Derek Powell, South Africa
Adriano Previtali, Switzerland
Balraj Puri, India
Paul Rabbat, Australia
H. Ramchandran, India
Fernando Rezende, Brazil
Horst Risse, Germany
Heather Roberts, Australia
Eduardo C. Robreno, United States

Rocío Arleth Rodríguez Torres, Mexico
Vladimir Rusinov, Russia
Marat Salikov, Russia
Alexander Salomatkin, Russia
Cheryl Saunders, Australia
Peter Savitski, Russia
Rekha Saxena, India
Anthony Sayers, Canada
Nicolas Schmitt, Switzerland
Hans-Peter Schneider, Germany
Rainer-Olaf Schultze, Germany
Pierre Scyboz, Switzerland
Campbell Sharman, Canada
Ronli Sifiris, Australia
Ajay K. Singh, India
Chhatar Singh, India
M.P. Singh, India
Khalipile Sizani, South Africa
Celina Souza, Brazil
Yuri Skuratov, Russia
Donald Speagle, Australia
David Stewart, Canada
Nico Steytler, South Africa
Kumar Suresh, India
Faiz Tajuddin, India
Fauzaya Talhaoui, Belgium

G. Alan Tarr, United States
Maria Hermínia Tavares de Almeida, Brazil
Paul Thomas, Canada
Krisztina Toth, Switzerland
Anne Twomey, Australia
A.A. Ujo, Nigeria
Bala Usman, Nigeria
Marnix Van Damme, Belgium
Oscar Vega Marín, Mexico
Francois Venter, South Africa
Ludo Veny, Belgium
Magali Verdonck, Belgium
Andrey Vikharev, Russia
Oscar Vilhena, Brazil
Bernhard Waldmann, Switzerland
Kristen Walker, Australia
Adam Wand, Australia
Ronald L. Watts, Canada
Bernard Wicht, Switzerland
Robert F. Williams, United States
George Winterton, Australia
Lisa Young, Canada
Elman Yusubov, Russia
Vladimir Zadiora, Russia
Mikhail Zatsepin, Russia
Emilio Zebadúa González, Mexico

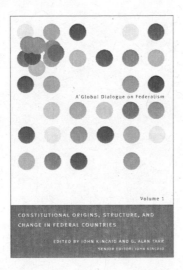

Constitutional Origins, Structure, and Change in Federal Countries
Edited by John Kincaid and G. Alan Tarr

Published for the Forum of Federations and the International Association of Centers for Federal Studies (IACFS)
Global Dialogue on Federalism Series

"This illuminating book is the written equivalent of listening to the wisdom of experience of other federal countries."
Dr Arnold Koller, former president of Switzerland

Providing examples of diverse forms of federalism, including new and mature, developed and developing, parliamentary and presidential, and common law and civil law, the comparative studies in this volume analyse government in Australia, Belgium, Brazil, Canada, Germany, India, Mexico, Nigeria, Russia, South Africa, Switzerland, and the United States. Each chapter describes the provisions of a constitution, explains the political, social, and historical factors that influenced its creation, and explores its practical application, how it has changed, and future challenges, offering valuable ideas and lessons for federal constitution-making and reform.

JOHN KINCAID is professor of Government and Public Service and director of the Robert B. and Helen S. Meyner Center for the Study of State and Local Government at Lafayette College.

G. ALAN TARR is director of the Center for State Constitutional Studies and chair of the Department of Political Science at Rutgers University-Camden.
A French edition of this book, *Les origines, structure, et changements constitutionnels dans les pays fédéraux*, will be available in fall 2005.

0-7735-2916-0 paper
0-7735-2849-0 cloth
6 x 9 480 pp 13 maps

Handbook of Federal Countries, 2005
Edited by Ann L. Griffiths, Coordinated by Karl Nerenberg

*An indispensable reference book on the developments, political dynamics,
institutions, and constitutions of the world's federal countries.*

Published for the Forum of Federations

For more than two centuries federalism has provided an example of how people can live
together even as they maintain their diversity. The *Handbook of Federal Countries, 2005*
continues the tradition started by the 2002 edition, updating and building on the work
of Ronald Watts and Daniel Elazar in providing a comparative examination of countries
organized on the federal principle.

Unique in its timely scope and depth, this volume includes a foreword by Forum
president Bob Rae that reflects on the importance of the federal idea in the
contemporary world. New comparative chapters examine the recent draft constitutional
treaty in Europe and the possibility of federalism being adopted in two countries with
longstanding violent conflicts – Sri Lanka and Sudan.

As a project of the Forum of Federations, an international network on federalism in
practice, the 2005 handbook is an essential sourcebook of information, with maps and
statistical tables in each chapter.

ANN GRIFFITHS is professor, Dalhousie College of Continuing Education, Dalhousie
University.
KARL NERENBERG is director of public information and senior editor, Forum of
Federations.

0-7735-2888-1
6 x 9 488pp 30 maps
French edition: *Guide des pays fédéraux, 2005*
0-7735-2896-2
6 x 9 536 pp 30 maps

Federalism in a Changing World
Learning from Each Other
Edited by Raoul Blindenbacher and Arnold Koller

A comprehensive overview of current issues in federalism.

Federalism in a Changing World contains the scientific background papers, proceedings, and plenary speeches presented at the International Conference on Federalism 2002 held in St Gallen, Switzerland, in August 2002. The three principal topics of the conference were federalism and foreign relations; federalism, decentralization, and conflict management in multicultural societies; and assignment of responsibilities and fiscal federalism. The volume comprises texts by more than seventy authors from twenty countries throughout the world.

RAOUL BLINDENBACHER is vice president, Forum of Federations, and former executive director of the International Conference on Federalism, 2002.
ARNOLD KOLLER is the former president of the Swiss Confederation and president of the Board of Directors of the International Conference on Federalism 2002.

0-7735-2603-x paper
0-7735-2602-1 cloth
6 x 9 617pp